Principles and Standar Navigations Series

NAVIGATING

through

PROBABILITY

in

GRADES 9–12

J. Michael Shaughnessy
Gloria Barrett
Rick Billstein
Henry A. Kranendonk
Roxy Peck

Johnny W. Lott
Grades 9–12 Editor

Peggy A. House
Navigations Series Editor

NATIONAL COUNCIL OF
TEACHERS OF MATHEMATICS

ISBN   0-87353-525-1

The National Council of Teachers of Mathematics is a public voice of mathematics education, providing vision, leadership, and professional development to support teachers in ensuring mathematics learning of the highest quality for all students.

Printed in the United States of America

NAVIGATIONS SERIES

TABLE OF CONTENTS

CONTENTS OF THE CD-ROM

Introduction to the Standard

Table of Standards and Expectations, Data Analysis and Probability, Pre-K–12

Applets

Binomial Distribution Simulator

Geometric Distribution Simulator

Random Number Generator

Adjustable Spinner

Prob Sim (for Macintosh)

Blackline Masters and Templates

Readings from Publications of the National Council of Teachers of Mathematics

A Program to Simulate the Galton Quincunx
Joseph Hilsenrath and Bruce F. Field
Mathematics Teacher

Representing Probabilities with Pipe Diagrams
Clifford Konold
Mathematics Teacher

Teaching Probability through Modeling Real Problems
Clifford Konold
Mathematics Teacher

Area Models and Expected Value
Glenda Lappan, Elizabeth Phillips, William M. Fitzgerald, and M. J. Winter
Mathematics Teacher

Data and Chance
    Judith S. Zawojewski and J. Michael Shaughnessy
    Results from the Seventh Mathematics Assessment of the National Assessment of Educational Progress

Readings and Classroom Materials from Other Sources

Lesson 1: Relative Frequency; Lesson 2: Applying Relative Frequency; Lesson 3: Designing a Simulation; Lesson 4: Waiting for Success; Lesson 6: Compound Events; Lesson 7: Complementary Events; and Lesson 8: Conditional Probability
    Patrick Hopfensperger, Henry Kranendonk, and Richard Scheaffer
    Data-Driven Mathematics: Probability through Data

It's Okay to Believe in the "Hot Hand"
    Patrick D. Larkey, Richard A. Smith, and Joseph B. Kadane
    Chance

Checker-A Game and Checker-B Game
    J. Michael Shaughnessy and Michael Arcidiacono
    Visual Encounters with Chance: Math and the Mind's Eye, Unit VIII

About This Book

This book provides a rationale and activities for exploring some of the "big ideas" of probability with high school students. Terms and definitions are introduced throughout, both in the discussion and in the examples and activities. The following major topics in probability are addressed:

- Introduction—the role and importance of probability
- Chapter 1—probability as long-run relative frequency
- Chapter 2—determining probability through an analysis of outcomes
- Chapter 3—independence and conditional probability
- Chapter 4—moving from sample spaces to probability distributions
- Chapter 5—expected value as "average" behavior in the long run

Activities explore and develop the main ideas in the book. Activity pages for students appear in the appendix as reproducible blackline masters, along with solutions to the problems presented. These blackline activity pages, which are signaled in the text by an icon, can also be printed from the CD-ROM that accompanies the book.

In addition to the blackline masters, the CD-ROM features special computer applets that complement the ideas in the text and activities. Teachers can let students use the applets in conjunction with particular activities, to facilitate the collection of data, or apart from the activities, to extend and deepen students' understanding.

The CD-ROM also includes readings for teachers' professional development, as well as supplemental materials for use in the classroom. A second icon in the text alerts readers to materials that appear on the CD-ROM.

Throughout the book, margin notes supply teaching tips, suggestions about related materials on the CD-ROM, and pertinent statements from *Principles and Standards for School Mathematics.* A third icon alerts the reader to these statements, which highlight relevant expectations for students in the area of probability, as articulated in NCTM's Data Analysis and Probability Standard.

Key to Icons

Blackline Master

CD-ROM

Principles and Standards

Three different icons appear in the book, as shown in the key. One signals the blackline masters and indicates their locations in the appendix, another points readers to supplementary materials on the CD-ROM that accompanies the book, and a third alerts readers to material quoted from *Principles and Standards for School Mathematics.*

NAVIGATING *through* PROBABILITY

Introduction

Probability is an area of the school mathematics curriculum that high school courses often gloss over or sometimes even skip. However, the importance of probabilistic reasoning—particularly, reasoning about the relationship between data and probability—has received increased attention from national groups over the past several decades (National Advisory Committee on Mathematical Education [NACOME] 1975; National Council of Teachers of Mathematics [NCTM] 1980; NCTM 1989).

In 1989, NCTM's *Curriculum and Evaluation Standards for School Mathematics* (NCTM 1989) accorded to probability and statistics the same status in the K–12 mathematics curriculum as algebra, geometry, measurement, and number and operations. Eleven years later, *Principles and Standards for School Mathematics* (NCTM 2000) reaffirmed this assessment of the importance of data analysis and probability in the pre-K–12 mathematics curriculum. In recognizing data and chance as key areas of the school mathematics curriculum, *Principles and Standards* recommends that content designed to develop statistical and probabilistic thinking be incorporated into the mathematics curriculum at all levels, for all students. The goal of such instruction is to enable all students from prekindergarten through grade 12 to "understand and apply basic concepts of probability" (NCTM 2000, p. 48).

Principles and Standards (p. 324) expects students in grades 9–12 to be able to—

• understand the concepts of sample space and probability distribution and construct sample spaces and distributions in simple cases;

- use simulations to construct empirical probability distributions;
- compute and interpret the expected value of random variables in simple cases;
- understand the concepts of conditional probability and independent events;
- understand how to compute the probability of a compound event.

We address these expectations throughout *Navigating through Probability in Grades 9–12*. Considering *why* it is important for students to learn about probability can serve as a useful prelude to this navigation through probability.

Why Study Probability?

In many situations in everyday life, we find ourselves thinking about whether a particular event is likely to occur, and if so, how likely it is to occur.

Chance is all around us—we do not live in a totally deterministic world

Weather prediction models are probabilistic in nature. Estimates of the likelihood of certain weather conditions (e.g., sun, rain, snow, wind, clouds) are based in part on satellite information about prevailing weather patterns and in part on knowledge of what has happened under similar conditions in the past. Predictions use percentages calculated from weather records stored in large databases.

Predictions about whether or not people will have a certain trait, such as brown eyes or brown hair, or a defective gene predisposing them to a certain disease, such as sickle-cell anemia, rely on probability. The probability of any of these occurrences is an estimate of its likelihood, and such an estimate involves an analysis of the prevalence of the particular genetic trait in a given population.

A myriad of circumstances give rise to questions about the likelihood of outcomes. The incidence and spread of communicable diseases, such as flu viruses, measles, and the common cold, can be represented with probability models. Court cases increasingly use arguments that are based on considerations of chance, especially with the advent of DNA evidence and the recognition that the probability of two identical strands of DNA coming from different people is very, very small. Decisions about where and whom to search at airports may depend on probabilistic information. Americans spend millions of dollars annually playing lotteries although their chances of winning are extremely small.

Unlike the certainty that characterizes algebraic calculations or geometric deductions, uncertainty—chance—affects our lives in ways that at times seem random or beyond our control. Why should we spend time considering whether an event that is not certain is likely to occur and how likely it is?

People must make decisions in the face of uncertainty

Doctors prescribe treatments or procedures for their patients, and often their recommendations are based on probabilistic information, such as data that show that treatment A has relieved condition B in x percent of similar cases in the past. Doctors' diagnoses have a probabilistic character, based on the likelihood that certain symptoms forecast particular disease possibilities.

Judges, juries, lawyers, and police officers often make decisions and recommendations in civil and criminal proceedings on the basis of bits and pieces of evidence that involve likelihood and chance.

Economists use data from the past, along with "likely" trends, to build economic models to predict, project, warn, and analyze. All these models use ideas about chance.

Pollsters and political analysts use data and chance in their estimates of the numbers and demographics of citizens who believe in particular issues or will vote for particular people.

Because chance and uncertainty are everywhere, an understanding of the basic elements of probability is essential to help students become well-informed citizens and to give them access to the many jobs and professions in which probability plays a crucial role.

Probability is indispensable for analyzing data; data are indispensable for estimating probabilities

In many of the examples cited, predictions and decisions about uncertain events involve an interplay between probability concepts and actual data. Doctors, judges, pollsters, meteorologists, and economists often appeal to the past, looking for what they can discover from the data on hand. Information available to decision makers may be based on past success rates or on probability estimates obtained from new or simulated data.

In addition, information obtained from a sample often supports inferences about what one might expect in the larger population from which the sample was drawn. Thus, decision makers can use data to estimate probabilities, which they can in turn use to make predictions from data. The importance of this interplay between data and chance for school mathematics cannot be overstated. The interconnection between data and probability is fundamental to this book, and it is paramount for school mathematics. The focus of interest is not so much probability for its own sake but rather the *relationships between probability and data.*

Questions That Involve Chance and Data

Consider the following four examples of questions that involve uncertainty or chance. How might someone begin to answer questions such as these?

1. What is the chance of an auto accident occurring at a complicated intersection?
2. What is the chance that a boy will develop hair loss if his father did?
3. What is the chance that a baseball player will get two hits in three consecutive batting attempts?
4. What is the chance that the stock market will go up three days in a row?

To investigate the chance of an accident at an intersection, members of a traffic safety review board might look at all the available data on accidents at the intersection. What was the record from the past? If they suspected that conditions were becoming more dangerous at the intersection, they might ask that a camera be installed to gather new data. With the help of either archival information or new data, they might be able to get an estimate of the number of accidents per number of cars passing through the intersection, or the number of accidents per unit of time.

A boy's chance of losing hair as an adult involves genetics. He is more likely to suffer hair loss if his father did. Estimates of the probability that a boy would develop hair loss if his father did might be based on genetic models, but the genetic models themselves might in turn be based on real data on the incidence of hair loss in families.

A baseball player's batting average is usually given as a decimal fraction (to three places), calculated by dividing the player's number of hits by his or her number of official times at bat. A baseball analyst could treat that average as fixed through three batting turns and use it as the probability that the player would get a hit in one at-bat. The analyst could then calculate probabilities for all the possible numbers of hits in three successive turns at bat for the player. Activities in the book explore this process.

As for the behavior of the stock market—who knows? The models that economists build to predict it take into account all sorts of variables—for example, unemployment rates, productivity indices, and the past history of the market under similar circumstances. The resulting theoretical models may help market analysts predict whether the stock market will go up or down, but an amateur observer might obtain an equally useful probability estimate by watching the stock market over a one-year period. He or she might count the number of three-day runs upward and divide by the total possible number of three-day runs in the year, thus obtaining an estimate of the probability of a three-day rise from actual data.

Approaches to Determining Probabilities

In considering approaches to questions such as these, two things are evident. First, all the questions lead to considerations of both data and chance. Second, when determining probabilities, people use one of two approaches. Sometimes they estimate probabilities from actual or simulated data, by using relative frequencies (as for the questions about traffic accidents and the stock market). In other situations, people compute probabilities by analyzing the possible outcomes theoretically and relying on previously "known" probabilities (as for the questions about hair loss and batting in baseball).

Introducing Probability

Statements of probability appear frequently in newspapers and magazines. Educated readers should be able to understand how reported probabilities, such as the probability of being struck by lightning, of being involved in an automobile accident, or of winning the lottery, have been determined and can be interpreted. Students need to develop an understanding of basic concepts of probability so that they can reason successfully about uncertain events, assess risks, and grasp the logic of making decisions in the presence of uncertainty.

Teachers can use the activity Is It Fair? as a preassessment of their students' thinking about probability.

Depending on your students' previous backgrounds and exposure to probability, they may talk about uncertainty, or chance, in various ways. They may speak of odds (e.g., 50-50), percentages (50 percent of the time), fractions (1/2), decimals (.5), or perhaps even something involving subjective beliefs that they cannot quantify in any way.

Before your students encounter the definitions and principles of probability in this book, you might want them to work through the introductory activity, Is It Fair? This activity is intended to give you an opportunity to assess your students' initial ideas about probability and a chance to introduce a probability simulation package (software or calculator).

Is it Fair?

Goals

- Explore individual beliefs and intuitions about a chance situation
- Explore a simple chance situation and compare two approaches—one using relative frequencies and the other using an analysis of outcomes

pp. 63–64

Materials and Equipment

- A copy of the activity pages for each student
- A pair of spinners, divided into shaded and white halves, for each pair of students
- Random Number Generator applet, simulation software or graphing calculators with simulation applications, Binomial Distribution Simulator applet, or Adjustable Spinner applet

p. 62

Patterns for spinners for Is It Fair? are available on the blackline master "Spinner Templates for 'Is It Fair?'"

Discussion

The question of fairness often arises in problems, games, or other situations involving chance. In fact, considerations of fairness can be good motivators for students of all ages when they are exploring chance. The activity Is It Fair? presents a spinner problem that is similar to one that appeared on the 1996 National Assessment of Education Progress (NAEP) and was subsequently released to the public. The item was administered exclusively to grade 12 students.

The problem involved two spinners, each divided into black and white halves. (For clarity and reproducibility, the black halves of the spinners have been shown here as shaded.) To win a carnival game with the spinners, a player must spin black on both spinners in single spins of each. The test item, which stated that James thought this would happen half the time, asked the twelfth-grade test-takers to say whether they agreed with James. Only 8 percent of the NAEP students correctly answered no to this question and reasoned correctly to support their answer (Zawojewski and Shaughnessy 2000). An additional 10 percent of the students reasoned that it would be half if there were only one spinner, so it should be something less for two spinners.

In a convenience sample of over 300 twelfth-grade NAEP students, more than half the students agreed with James that there was a 50-50 chance of both spinners landing on black. Most students who reasoned that the game was fair wrote that "half the area is black" or "there are two blacks out of four regions" (Shaughnessy and Zawojewski 1999, p. 716). Only 21 twelfth graders in the convenience sample actually listed the outcomes (BW, BB, WB, WW). An additional 24 students used some sort of multiplication principle to reason correctly that the chance of both spinners landing on black was only 25 percent, or 1/4.

The responses to this NAEP problem suggest that many grade 12 students need an introduction to probability. The problem appears to yield a variety of intuitive responses and makes the task of generating actual data relatively easy, either with actual spinners or simulations. After asking students to write down their initial thinking about the

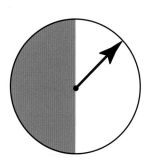

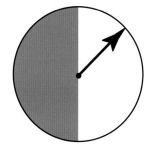

6

spinner problem, the activity asks them to predict how many times they would expect to win if they played the game 10 times. Then, working in pairs, they gather data for 10 games. Students can make spinners by using the templates on the blackline master "Spinner Templates for 'Is It Fair?'" with paper clips as spinner arrows. They can straighten one end of a paper clip, put a pencil point through the still-looped end of the clip, and use the point to anchor the straightened clip at the center of a spinner disk, as shown in the sketch in the margin. Alternatively, students can use a random number generator, letting 0–4 stand for a spinner landing in the shaded area and 5–9 stand for a spinner landing on white.

It is beneficial to have students start the activity Is It Fair? by spinning real spinners, because this process helps them "see" the four possible outcomes for the game when they are gathering their data. A pedagogical limitation of simulation software and calculator probability packages is that their speed can mask what is happening. Having students actually spin spinners can be a more powerful approach, especially at first.

After gathering data from 10 games, students may change their minds about their original answer to the question. The data from several sets of 10 games usually do not support the position that the game is fair, or that the chance of both spinners landing in the shaded area is 50-50, as James believed. Figures 0.1a through 0.1d show frequency graphs for 10, 20, 50, and 100 plays of the game. In the long run, landing two spinners in shaded areas clearly does not occur 50 percent of the time.

As a final step in this activity, you might ask students to list the possible outcomes for the spinner task and to assign probabilities to them. (This approach is presented in detail in chapter 2). All students are unlikely to agree on the outcomes to list, so it may be beneficial for them to share their thinking about this task. Then ask the students to compare the relative-frequency information (proportions) that they collected from their spinners or simulations to the probabilities that they assigned to the outcomes on their lists.

Students who initially believed that the chance of both spinners landing in the shaded areas was 50-50 might list the outcomes as "both shaded" or "not both shaded" and believe that these two outcomes are equally likely. The data contradict this position.

Students who initially believed that there must be "less than a 50-50 chance, because the chance would be half if there were only one spinner," might list the outcomes "both shaded," "both white," and "one shaded and one white." The data will show that these three outcomes are not equally likely—each of them does not have a 1/3 chance of occurring.

Usually there are several students who will argue correctly that there are four outcomes and that each has a 1/4 chance of occurring. They can find powerful support for this analysis in the data obtained from the relative-frequency approach that they used in experimenting with the spinners.

Probability as a Tool for Describing Behavior in the Long Run

By examining relative frequencies of outcomes as students have done with the pairs of spinners in Is It Fair? they can gain a sense of probability as the likelihood of an event in the long run. The following chapters elaborate this interpretation of probability.

See the accompanying CD-ROM for Zawojewski and Shaughnessy's (2000) discussion of twelfth graders' responses to the spinner question on the 1996 NAEP.

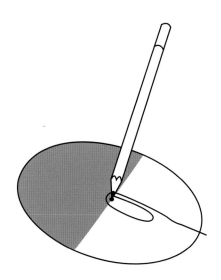

Having students begin by spinning real spinners instead of using a simulation can make the possible outcomes very concrete.

The CD-ROM includes a Random Number Generator applet that can be used with this and other activities in the book.

Fig. **0.1.**

Frequency graphs for sets of games with
the two spinners

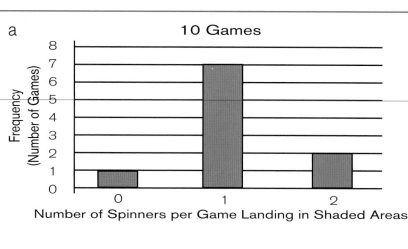

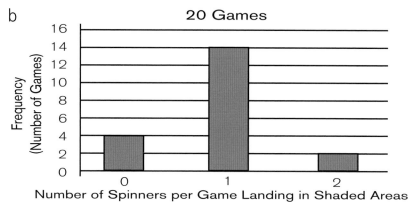

*The Adjustable
Spinner applet
on the CD-*
*ROM can help students
understand the probabilities
associated with spinners.
The applet's virtual spinner
shows one to nine sectors of
varying colors and angle
measures, and the applet
tallies and displays the
results of virtual spins. For
Is It Fair? students can use
the applet to make a virtual
spinner with differently
colored halves, and then
they can collect data from
pairs of successive spins.*

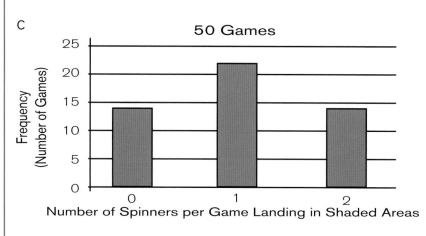

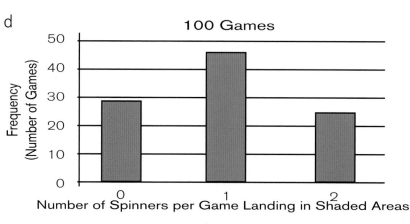

NAVIGATING *through* PROBABILITY

Chapter 1
Probability as Long-Run Relative Frequency

Throughout, this book applies the relative-frequency interpretation of probability and uses the long-run relative frequencies of outcomes to estimate probabilities directly and to explain and illustrate ways of assigning classical theoretical probabilities to outcomes.

Probability is the mathematician's attempt to measure uncertainty, or chance. Early work in probability focused on games of chance—games in which the outcome depends on a chance mechanism, such as the roll of a die, the toss of a coin, or the spin of a spinner, as in the carnival game in the introduction. People studying these games noticed that although there was uncertainty about the outcome of any particular play of the game, outcomes were predictable in the long run.

The possibility of describing and quantifying behavior in the long run, even when there is randomness in individual outcomes, leads to an understanding of probability known as the relative-frequency interpretation. According to this interpretation, the probability of an outcome is the proportion of time that the outcome will occur in the long run.

The following activity, Spinning in Circles, develops students' understanding of this interpretation of probability as they examine the relative frequency of an outcome over the long run.

Spinning in Circles

Goal

- Understand the concept of probability as the long-run relative frequency of an outcome

Materials and Equipment

- A copy of the activity pages for each student
- A small paper clip for each student

pp. 65–69

Discussion

This activity uses the spinner shown in a reduced size in figure 1.1 to introduce the idea of probability as a long-run relative frequency. When the spinner is spun, the tip of the arrow lands in either the white region or the shaded region.

Fig. 1.1.

The spinner (reduced in size) for the activity Spinning in Circles

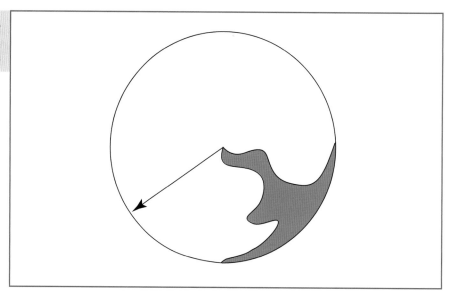

When opened, paper clips for Spinning in Circles should form spinner arrows that are equal in length to the radius (2 1/8 inches) of the spinner disk on the activity page. (The tip of the paper-clip spinner arrow should reach the spinner circle itself. A spinner arrow can be longer than the radius, if necessary, but not shorter.)

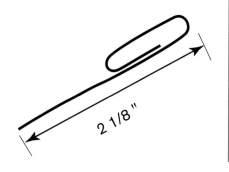

Even after working through the activity Is It Fair? students may still have unreliable intuitions about the probability of having the spinner given for this activity land in the shaded region. Some students might choose one-tenth as the probability of the spinner landing in the shaded area because it is small relative to the white area, even though one-fourth of the circumference of the circle is shaded, and the point of the arrow determines the outcome. Others might choose one-half because there are only two possible outcomes. These conclusions represent common errors that students make when first encountering ideas about probability.

The activity guides students in constructing two plots that show pairs of points (*Cumulative number of spins, Proportion of spins in the shaded region*) to illustrate the fact that although the proportion of "shaded" outcomes may behave erratically in the short run (as in the 20 spins that students show in plot 1; see the plot of sample data on p. 113), it does not continue to jump around as the number of spins increases. In the long run (as in the large number of spins that students show in plot 2; see the plot of sample data on page 114), the relative frequency of an outcome settles down, eventually becoming close to the true probability of that outcome.

In the activity Spinning in Circles, students see that the long-run relative frequency of spins landing in the shaded region stabilizes, eventually becoming close to—and staying close to—the true probability of the occurrence of that outcome. The relative-frequency interpretation of probability provides a convenient strategy for estimating probabilities empirically by using an observed relative frequency of an outcome in the long run. In some instances, it is possible to use a simulation to generate the observations to estimate a probability. This approach is illustrated in the following activity, A Matter of Taste.

Simulation can be a useful tool for estimating probabilities.

A Matter of Taste

Goals

- Illustrate the use of simulation to investigate frequencies of outcomes
- Use an observed relative frequency to estimate a probability
- Use probability as the basis for making a decision

Materials and Equipment

- A copy of the activity pages for each pair of students
- A small paper bag for each pair of students
- Two chips, one labeled "A" and the other labeled "B," for each pair of students

pp. 70–72

Discussion

The activity A Matter of Taste helps students build on their newly acquired understanding of the long-run relative-frequency interpretation of probability. Extending ideas from the activity Spinning in Circles, A Matter of Taste shows students how they can use an observed relative frequency to estimate a probability.

In the activity, students use a simulation to examine a scenario in which Jessica contends that she can correctly identify cola A and cola B by their taste. Jessica's friend Luke is skeptical of her claim, so Jessica asks him to put it to a test by randomly selecting one of the colas, pouring it into a paper cup, and giving it to her to taste and identify. Jessica correctly names the cola presented to her in two tests.

Students work in pairs to investigate the likelihood that Jessica actually could not distinguish colas A and B but happened to make two lucky guesses in a row. Within each pair, one student takes the role of Jessica and the other takes the role of Luke in a simulation of the cola-tasting trials. Two chips, one labeled "A" and the other labeled "B," represent cola A and cola B. The student playing Luke puts the chips into a paper bag, shakes it, and draws out a chip without letting the student playing Jessica see which chip it is. Jessica guesses whether it is chip A or chip B, simulating an attempt to guess the cola without really being able to tell one cola from the other.

This simulation gives the students an opportunity to discover that, in two tests of the colas, Jessica would be giving one of four possible responses—AA, AB, BA, BB. Only one of these responses would correspond to correct identifications in both attempts, and, with Jessica just guessing, all four responses would be equally likely. Thus, the true value of the probability that the students estimate in the first part of the activity is .25.

It is useful for students to combine the data gathered by all the student pairs to examine the class estimate of this value. The activity asks the students to do this in step 3. If you have a small class, you may need to have each pair of students complete more than twenty trials to obtain a reasonable estimate. You may want to list each pair's proportion from

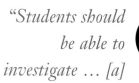

"Students should be able to investigate ... [a] question by using a simulation to obtain an approximate answer."
(NCTM 2000, p. 333)

Suppose Jessica happened to be just guessing and could not actually distinguish between cola **A** and cola **B**. What would be the probability of Jessica making two lucky correct guesses in a row? How many times might Jessica need to name the cola correctly twice in a row to convince Luke that she really could distinguish between cola **A** and cola **B**?

step 2 on the board, along with the estimate based on the combined data from the entire class.

You might want to point out to the students that after just twenty trials the estimates may vary quite a bit—both from one another and from the actual probability of .25. The estimate based on a larger number of trials (the combined class data) should be fairly close to .25. This is a consequence of the cumulative stabilization of the relative frequency, a phenomenon that the students discovered in the activity Spinning in Circles.

The questions posed in the Discussion and Extension section of the activity probe how many times Jessica might need to identify cola samples correctly before Luke became convinced that she really could distinguish between cola A and cola B. Students' work on this section helps them see how a calculation of probabilities can contribute to an informed decision. Students often decide that being correct on each of 4 or 5 tests should convince Luke that Jessica really can distinguish between the two brands of cola.

The activity A Matter of Taste shows students how they can estimate the probability of a particular outcome empirically in some cases. In other cases, they might be interested in some numerical aspect of the outcome, rather than in the outcome itself. The following activity, One-Boy Family Planning, illustrates such a case.

The cumulative stabilization of the relative frequency of an outcome in a large number of trials makes it a good estimate of the probability of the outcome.

One-Boy Family Planning

Goals

- ~~Use probability to describe the behavior of a variable in the long run~~
- Set the stage for later work with probability distributions

Materials and Equipment

- A copy of the activity pages for each student
- A six-sided die for each student

pp. 73–75

Discussion

In this activity, students consider a variation on China's one-child population policy. They examine a hypothetical policy that would allow families to continue having children until they produced a boy. Students use a simulation to collect data and calculate the observed relative frequencies of small and large sibling groups under such a policy. The simulation allows students to use probability to investigate the consequences of a revision sometimes suggested by citizens in rural China to their country's one-child family-planning policy. Instead of restricting Chinese couples to one child, the proposed revision would restrict them to one son.

The students use a roll of a six-sided die to simulate the birth of a child, with an even-numbered outcome (2, 4, or 6) representing the birth of a girl and an odd-numbered outcome (1, 3, or 5) representing the birth of a boy. Individual rolls of the die have equal chances of results that represent girls and results that represent boys. Although the proportion of male births is actually slightly higher than .5 in the human population, it is sufficiently close to .5 that this way of simulating a birth is reasonable. The students continue to roll the die until a "sibling group"—the set of children allowed to a family according to a one-boy policy—is complete.

Each student generates twenty simulated sibling groups in this way to investigate the behavior of the variable *Sibling group size* under a one-boy policy of family planning. Then all the students combine their data to approximate the distribution of sibling groups by size. If you have fewer than twenty students, you may want to have each student form more than twenty sibling groups to ensure that your students will have a sufficiently large number of observations to get a reasonable approximation for the distribution of sibling groups by size.

A convenient way to create the class distribution of sibling groups by size is to list family sizes in a column on the board and then let your students come up and enter tally marks for each of their twenty observations. You are unlikely to see any sibling groups larger than size 8 or size 9 under the one-boy policy, but it might be a good idea to mention that this is not because larger family sizes would be impossible but because they would be extremely rare.

See "Teaching Probability through Modeling Real Problems" (Konold 1994) on the accompanying CD-ROM for additional ideas.

You may want to form a few simulated sibling groups to model the process before students begin work on the activity. For example, if you happened to roll the following sequence of numbers:

6 → Girl, 2 → Girl, 3 → Boy,

your students should understand that the simulated birth of a boy would complete the simulated sibling group GGB, and the sibling group size would be 3.

This activity is based on Konold 1994.

In the final part of the activity, students convert their observed frequencies (counts) to relative frequencies (proportions), which they then use to answer questions about the likelihood of sibling groups of various sizes. This work builds on the ideas introduced in the activity A Matter of Taste.

Conclusion

This chapter has set the stage for what follows in our investigation of probability in grades 9–12 by introducing three fundamental ideas:

- Probability can be thought of as the relative frequency of an occurrence in the long run.
- Probabilities can be estimated empirically.
- Probability can be used to describe the behavior of a variable in the long run.

These ideas have been illustrated in the activities Spinning in Circles, A Matter of Taste, and One-Boy Family Planning, respectively, and they will be revisited more formally in the chapters that follow.

Chapter 5 gives students an opportunity to study the behavior of the variable Sibling group size *more formally in a related activity, One-Girl Family Planning.*

NAVIGATING *through* PROBABILITY

Chapter 2
Sample Spaces

Principles and Standards for School Mathematics recommends that all students in grades 9–12 should—

- understand the concepts of sample space and … construct sample spaces … in simple cases; … [and]
- understand how to compute the probability of a compound event (NCTM 2000, p. 324).

This chapter explores these two probability expectations for high school students.

Chapter 1 defined and discussed probability as the long-run relative frequency of an outcome, and the activities treated the probability of an outcome as the proportion of time that the outcome occurred in many repetitions over time. In general, this approach involves performing an experiment (such as spinning a spinner or flipping a coin or pulling a colored candy out of a bag), or simulating the experiment, again and again, recording the results, and calculating the proportion of time that the outcome occurs.

However, there are some situations in which one has an idea in advance about the proportion of time that a particular outcome will occur. For example, the probability of getting tails on a flip of a coin is easily seen to be 1/2, or 50 percent, because there are clearly two outcomes, heads (H) and tails (T). (Note that having a coin land on its edge is so uncommon that no one even considers its probability.) If the coin is fair, each outcome has an equal chance of occurring when the coin is flipped many, many times.

Imagine a paper bag containing 3 blue, 2 yellow, 3 green, and 4 red candies, identical in every respect except color. This is a slightly less obvious but still simple situation. If you were blindfolded and drew out a candy, what would be your chance of drawing a red one? Someone might argue, incorrectly, that because there are four outcomes for this experiment—red, yellow, green, or blue—red would have a 1/4 chance of occurring. However, all the colors would not have the same chance of being drawn, because there are more candies of some colors than of others. Because 4 out of 12 candies are red, the chance of getting a red candy would be 4 out of 12, for a probability of 4/12, or 1/3.

In analyzing the situation involving either the flipping of the coin or the selecting of a piece of candy, you could list all the possible outcomes and then assign probabilities to each on the basis of some reasonable argument. If you wished, you could test how well your assigned probabilities worked by conducting an experiment and comparing the long-term proportions with your predictions.

Sample Space

In simple probability experiments such as the coin toss or the candy selection, it is possible and feasible to list all the outcomes and assign probabilities to each of them. Listing all the possible outcomes for a probability experiment can be a great help in understanding what might happen and why some outcomes would occur more frequently than others. The set of all possible outcomes for a probability experiment is the *sample space* for the experiment. It is useful to consider a sample space of outcomes as a *set*. Set notation provides a convenient way to represent subsets of outcomes from the sample space.

The sample space for flipping a fair coin is {H, T}, where H represents obtaining a head and T represents obtaining a tail. The sample space for the candy example above is {B, Y, G, R}, where B represents obtaining a blue candy; Y, a yellow candy; R, a red candy; and G, a green candy. In the candy example, the probability of drawing a red candy is 4/12, denoted by $P(R) = 4/12$. Similarly, $P(Y) = 2/12$, and $P(B) = 3/12$, and $P(G) = 3/12$. The sum of all the probabilities of the outcomes in a sample space is 1.

The Addition Principles

In the example of selecting candy from a paper bag, we can add the individual probabilities of selecting a red candy and selecting a blue candy to find the probability of the event "selecting either a red candy or a blue candy." Using set notation, we can write what we are doing as $P(R \text{ or } B) = P(R \cup B) = P(R) + P(B) = 4/12 + 3/12 = 7/12$.

Straight addition of probabilities works only in cases where the two events have nothing in common—that is, when the events are *mutually exclusive*. If two events from a sample space have no common outcomes, the probability of either one or the other occurring is the sum of their individual probabilities. This relationship is known as the *addition principle for mutually exclusive events* and can be expressed symbolically in the following way:

If A and B are two events in a sample space and $A \cap B = \varnothing$, then $P(A \text{ or } B) = P(A \cup B) = P(A) + P(B)$.

"Students should be able to describe sample spaces such as the set of possible outcomes when four coins are tossed and the set of possibilities for the sum of the values on the faces that are down when two tetrahedral dice are rolled."

(NCTM 2000, p. 331)

A *sample space* is the set of all possible outcomes for a probability experiment. An *event* in a probability experiment is a subset of the sample space. For example, getting either a red (R) or a blue (B) candy from a bag containing red, blue, yellow (Y), and green (G) candies is an event that can be denoted by {R} ∪ {B} = {R, B}. The event {R, B} is a subset of the whole sample space, {R, B, Y, G}.

The notation $P(R)$, rather than $P(\{R\})$, is used to denote the probability of the event R. Dropping the set notation is a common practice in denoting the probability of an event.

Suppose two events are *not* mutually exclusive. For instance, in the candy selection example, consider two events X and W, where X represents choosing either a red or a blue candy, and W represents choosing either a green or a blue candy. Thus, X = {R, B} and W = {G, B} in the sample space {B, Y, G, R}. The events X and W have a common element, B, so they are not mutually exclusive: $X \cap W = \{B\} \neq \emptyset$. Suppose that you are computing the probability of one event or the other happening—that is, $P(X \cup W)$. Then you must subtract the probability of their overlap—that is, $P(X \cap W)$—to avoid double counting. This idea is expressed in the *general addition principle*:

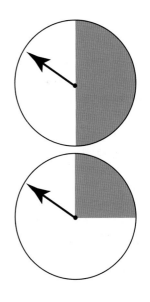

If A and B are any two events in a sample space,

then $P(\text{A or B}) = P(\text{A} \cup \text{B})$

$$= P(\text{A}) + P(\text{B}) - P(\text{A } and \text{ B})$$
$$= P(\text{A}) + P(\text{B}) - P(\text{A} \cap \text{B}).$$

In the candy selection example, you know that P(R) = 4/12, P(B) = 3/12, and P(G) = 3/12. If X = {R, B} and W = {G, B}, then X ∩ W = {B}. Although X and W are not mutually exclusive events, event X denotes mutually exclusive events, {R} and {B}, and event W denotes mutually exclusive events, {G} and {B}. Thus, you can find the probabilities of events X and W by using the addition principle for mutually exclusive events: $P(X) = P(R \cup B) = 4/12 + 3/12 = 7/12$, and $P(W) = P(B \cup G) = 3/12 + 3/12 = 6/12$. You can then use the general addition principle to find the probability of X or W: $P(X \cup W) = P(X) + P(W) - P(X \cap W) = 7/12 + 6/12 - 3/12 = 10/12$. If you did not subtract the 3/12 probability of selecting blue, you would have counted it twice.

The Multiplication Principles

The introductory activity Is It Fair? presented a problem involving two spinners, both of which were equally divided into white and shaded regions. The sample space for that problem was {SS, SW, WS, WW}, where S indicates a spinner that lands in a shaded region, and W indicates a spinner that lands on white. The first activity in chapter 2, Check Out *These* Spinners, revisits this problem, presenting a game that uses a different pair of spinners but has the same sample space. Here the four outcomes do not all have the same probability of occurring. In the new activity, one spinner is half shaded and half white, and the other is one-quarter shaded and three-quarters white. As in the spinner game in Is It Fair? players spin both spinners once and win if both spinners land in the shaded areas.

Thus, in both spinner problems, students can think of one round of the game as consisting of two spins, one after the other. Players spin the first spinner, and the outcome is either "shaded" or "white," with certain probabilities, and then they spin the second spinner, and again the outcome is either "shaded" or "white," with certain probabilities.

In probability, when outcomes occur in sequence, each one can be considered individually, or the sequence of outcomes can be considered as a whole. For example, in both Is It Fair? and Check Out *These* Spinners, SW denotes a sequence of two individual outcomes—"shaded" on the first spin, and "white" on the second. When outcomes occur in a sequence and are independent of one another, the probability of the

If $A \cap B = \emptyset$ for two events A and B in a sample space, then A and B are *mutually exclusive.*

"High school students should learn to identify mutually exclusive, joint, and conditional events."
(NCTM 2000, p. 331)

 "All students should … understand how to compute the probability of a compound event."
(NCTM 2000, p. 324)

sequence of outcomes is the product of the individual probabilities of the outcomes. This idea is expressed in the *multiplication principle for independent events:*

If A and B are two independent events that occur in succession, and $P(A) = r$ and $P(B) = s$, then the probability that A *and* B occur is $P(A \cap B) = r \cdot s$.

For example, in the activity Is It Fair? the probability that the first spinner will land in the shaded area is 1/2, and the probability that the second spinner will land in the shaded area is also 1/2. Thus, the probability that *both* spinners will land in the shaded area, one after the other, is "half of a half," or $1/2 \cdot 1/2 = 1/4$. Note that each additional outcome in a sequence of outcomes successively reduces the chance of the entire sequence occurring.

If two events occur in succession, the *general multiplication principle* applies whether the events are independent or not. This principle also addresses conditional probability. Imagine that events A and B occur in succession, but B can occur only if A occurs, as, for example, in the question "What is the probability that a randomly selected person is wearing blue (B), given that the person is eating an apple (A)?" In other words, A is a condition for B. The probability of A and B can then be expressed as $P(A \cap B) = P(A) \cdot P(B \text{ given } A)$. This relationship is customarily denoted as $P(A \cap B) = P(A) \cdot P(B \mid A)$. Conditional probability is considered in more detail in chapter 3.

Two outcomes are *independent* if the occurrence of one outcome does not change the probability of the other one.

See "Representing Probabilities with Pipe Diagrams" (Konold 1996) on the accompanying CD-ROM for a useful variation on tree diagrams for representing outcomes and determining sample spaces.

When events occur in sequence, the set notation A ∩ B, which indicates that both A and B have occurred, is abbreviated as AB. For example, in the spinner activity Is It Fair, the sequence of events "first spin in the shaded area" and "second spin in the shaded area" is written as SS, and $P(\text{SS}) = 1/2 \cdot 1/2$.

Check Out *These* Spinners

Goals

- Explore individual beliefs and intuitions about a chance situation
- Explore a simple chance situation and compare two approaches, one using relative frequencies to assign empirical probabilities and the other using an analysis of outcomes to assign theoretical probabilities
- Demonstrate the multiplication principle for independent events

Materials and Equipment

- A copy of the activity pages for each student
- A pair of spinners for each pair of students. (One spinner should be equally divided into shaded and white regions, and the other should have one quarter shaded and three quarters white.)

Discussion

When the students consider the new spinner game presented in this activity, some of them might think of each of the spinner circles as cut into quarters to form eight sectors of equal size, three of which are shaded. As a result, they might believe that the chance of both spinners landing in shaded areas would be 3/8. Other students might combine the areas of the shaded parts and compare them to the area of a single spinner, and as a result they might believe that the chance of both spinners landing on shaded areas would be 3/4. Still others might dispute this conclusion, arguing that the probability of both spinners landing in the shaded areas has to be less than it was in the first spinner game, where both spinners were half shaded and half white.

It is helpful to have students experiment with the spinners in pairs, gathering data from 50 games to get a good sense of the situation. Students can again make spinners by using paper clips as spinner arrows, anchoring them with pencils at the center of the spinner disks on the blackline master "Spinner Templates for 'Check Out *These* Spinners.'"

The activity Check Out *These* Spinners is designed to help students collect data that demonstrate the multiplication principle for independent events. Depending on the needs and backgrounds of your students, you can have them use the activity in one of two ways. They can carry out the simulation to discover and gather support for the multiplication principle, or you can discuss the multiplication principle with them first and have them carry out the simulation afterward to confirm the principle.

Note that you and your students might expect 1000 of 2000 spins of the first spinner to land in the shaded areas, but for only about 1/4 of those 1000 spins would you expect spins of the second spinner also to land in the shaded area, or about 1/4 of 1000, or 250 times out of 2000. You can begin to flesh out and give meaning to the multiplication principle for your students by talking through the problem in this way: "If we played the game 2000 times, about how many times would we expect the first spinner to land in the shaded area? Now, of those spins

pp. 77–78

Patterns for spinners are available on the blackline master "Spinner Templates for 'Check Out *These* Spinners.'"

p. 76

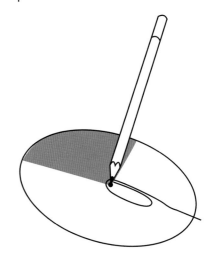

Students can experiment with the Adjustable Spinner applet on the CD-ROM to investigate results with virtual spinners that they configure like those in Check Out These *Spinners.*

in the shaded area on the first spinner, how many would we expect to be paired with spins in the shaded area on the second spinner?"

The next activity, Sounding an Alarm, gives students another opportunity to investigate probabilities of compound events.

Sounding an Alarm

Goals

- Explore individual beliefs and intuitions about probabilities of compound events
- Approach a chance situation involving compound events through an analysis of outcomes
- Verify the multiplication principle for independent events and the addition principle for mutually exclusive events and apply these principles

Materials and Equipment

- A copy of the activity pages for each student

Discussion

This activity presents students with the efforts of students at North High School to solve a problem involving independent events. The North High School students examined how likely it would be that at least one smoke detector would sound if smoke appeared in their school cafeteria, which was newly equipped with three smoke detectors, each with a 75 percent chance of sounding if smoke appeared anywhere in the room.

The North High School students listed the possible outcomes as {0S, 1S, 2S, 3S}, with 0S representing zero smoke detectors sounding, 1S representing one, 2S representing two, and 3S representing three smoke detectors sounding. They assigned the following probabilities to the outcomes: $P(0S) = 1/4$, $P(1S) = 1/4$, $P(2S) = 1/4$, and $P(3S) = 1/4$. Thus, assuming that there was a 1/4 probability that no smoke detector would sound if smoke appeared somewhere in the cafeteria, these students concluded incorrectly that the probability of at least one detector sounding would be $1 - 1/4$, or 3/4.

In working through the activity, your students must make a guess about the likelihood of an event that is quite nonintuitive. They must review the North High School students' approach to the problem and make actual calculations that they can compare with their own guesses. The activity also asks your students to generate their own sample space after critiquing the other students' approach.

This activity builds on and extends the activity Check Out *These Spinners* by introducing three outcomes that can be considered in succession. Both the multiplication principle for independent events and the addition principle for mutually exclusive events are needed to calculate probabilities for events in the sample space. After students make their own lists of outcomes, they should see that the probability of no smoke detector sounding would be $1/4 \cdot 1/4 \cdot 1/4$, or 1/64, and that the probability that at least one detector would sound would be $1 - 1/64$, or 63/64, or about .984.

In the next activity, Three-Dice Sums, students again examine their beliefs and intuitions about events that occur by chance.

pp. 79–80

The activity Sounding an Alarm presents students with three outcomes that can be considered in succession.

Three-Dice Sums

Goals

- Explore individual beliefs and intuitions about a chance situation
- Explore a simple chance situation and compare two approaches, one using relative frequencies and the other using an analysis of outcomes
- Apply both the multiplication principle for independent events and the addition principle for mutually exclusive events to a sample space

Materials and Equipment

- A copy of the activity pages for each student
- Three regular six-sided dice for each pair of students—three colors if possible
- A sheet of grid paper or a copy of the blackline master "Graph the Frequencies of Three-Dice Sums" for each pair of students and several extra sheets for the students to use in larger groups

pp. 81–82

The blackline master "Graph the Frequencies of Three-Dice Sums" provides a template for grid paper for the activity.

p. 83

Discussion

This activity offers a variation on the age-old problem of finding the probabilities of the sums of the numbers obtained by tossing a pair of dice. Here students toss three dice and consider the possible outcomes and their probabilities. Secondary students are unlikely to have good intuitions about the three-dice problem, so the activity can provide an opportunity for them to gather some data and compare them with calculations that use the addition and multiplication principles.

If possible, provide each group of students with dice in three colors. The different colors can help resolve arguments about the sample space for tossing three dice.

Students may be surprised to find how rare some of the smaller and larger sums are (for example, 3, 4, 5, 16, 17, 18). Of the 6 • 6 • 6, or 216, possible triples that result from tossing three dice, only one triple gives a sum of 3: (1, 1, 1). Three triples give a sum of 4: (1, 1, 2), (1, 2, 1), and (2, 1, 1); and so on. Thus, the probability of getting a sum of 3 with a toss of three dice is 1/216, or about .0046; the probability of getting a sum of 4 is 3/216, or about .0138; and so on.

This activity illustrates how *un*equal the likelihoods of outcomes can be in a probability experiment. It can persuade students that 36 sums are really possible in a two-dice probability experiment, and it can also help them see that in such an experiment outcomes like (2, 1) and (1, 2) are really different.

Students turn from their own experiments with three dice to a theoretical analysis of possible outcomes and conclude the activity by comparing this analysis with their work with relative frequencies. To make the comparison more meaningful, you might have your class pool the experimental data gathered by all the student pairs and use them to construct a whole-class frequency distribution.

Giving students differently colored dice helps them explore and understand the sample space for the sums of three dice.

Your students could compare the pooled distribution with their own distributions based on fewer data. (Be sure that they understand that calculating relative frequencies provides a basis for comparing data across distributions when the numbers of trials—that is, the sample sizes—are not the same for different groups.) Your students could also graph the theoretical distribution of three-dice sums and compare this perfectly symmetrical distribution (with modal values at 10 and 11) with their whole-class distribution. Frequency distributions based on actual tosses will have irregular peaks and valleys and will rarely be exactly symmetrical.

Conclusion

This chapter has probed theoretical probability and has shown how to introduce the concepts *sample space* and *event*. In working through the chapter's activities, students should have begun to see the long-term "convergence" of the relative frequencies of the outcomes of an experiment over many repeated trials of the experiment. In becoming aware of this eventual convergence, students should have begun to connect these long-run relative frequencies—sometimes called the "experimental probabilities"—with the theoretical probabilities of the outcomes in the sample space of a probability experiment. The chapter has also focused on giving students various tools for calculating probabilities of outcomes in sample spaces, such as the addition principle and the multiplication principle. The next chapter focuses on teaching about *independence* of events.

NAVIGATIONS SERIES

GRADES 9–12

NAVIGATING *through* PROBABILITY

Chapter 3
Independence and Conditional Probabilities

"All students should ... understand the concepts of conditional probability and independent events."
(NCTM 2000, p. 324)

A group of high school students developed the following questions for research:

- Of the student drivers at Waldo High School, are those whose parents have set a midnight curfew less likely to have received a ticket for a traffic violation than those whose parents have not set such a curfew?
- Are students who listen regularly to classical music likely to have higher grade-point averages than those who do not?
- Are male teenaged drivers more likely than female teenaged drivers to have been involved in a traffic accident?
- Do students with above-average SAT scores have a higher probability than students with below-average SAT scores of being successful in college?
- Is a child of parents who smoke more likely to have asthma than is a child of parents who do not smoke?
- Are left-handed people more likely than right-handed people to be interested in the arts?

This chapter provides a framework for organizing data and interpreting probabilities to explore these types of questions. To conduct such investigations, students need an understanding of the concept of independence.

As discussed in chapter 2, two events are *independent* if the occurrence of one of them does not change the likelihood of the occurrence of the

27

other. Whether or not two events are independent can be determined by interpreting probabilities.

For example, in the case of the first research question, consider a student driver selected at random from all the Waldo High School students with parents who have set a midnight curfew. What is the likelihood that this selected student has received a ticket for a traffic violation? Suppose that 15 percent of all the student drivers at Waldo High School have received tickets, but only 3 percent of the student drivers with curfews have received them. Then the likelihood that a selected Waldo High School student driver *with* a curfew has received a traffic ticket is not the same as the likelihood that a selected Waldo High School student driver, *with or without a curfew*, has received a traffic ticket.

The second event that we are interested in, "selecting a student driver with a ticket," is not independent of the occurrence of the first event, "selecting a student driver with a curfew." The selection of a Waldo High School student driver with a curfew affects—in this case, *decreases*—the likelihood that the student driver has received a ticket. Thus, the events are not independent.

If the events *were* independent, the proportion of Waldo High School student drivers whose parents had set curfews and who also had received tickets would be equal to the proportion of Waldo High School student drivers, with or without curfews, who had received tickets. In other words, *if* the likelihood of selecting a student driver who had a curfew and had received a ticket were *the same as* the likelihood of selecting a student driver who had received a ticket, without regard to the curfew, then the events would be independent.

Probabilities indicate whether or not events are independent. This chapter probes this idea while addressing the following three questions:

1. When are two events considered independent?
2. What is a conditional probability?
3. How can conditional probabilities be used to tell if two events are independent or not independent?

The chapter's investigation of independent events begins with the activity Abby's Kennels, which presents data on dogs' sizes (large or small) and their results in an obedience course (passed or did not pass). Students examine conditional probabilities as a way of determining whether the events "selecting a dog that is large [or small]" and "selecting a dog that passed [or did not pass] the course" are independent.

Abby's Kennels

Goal

- Use conditional probabilities to understand when two events are independent

Materials and Equipment

- A copy of the activity pages for each student
- A set of three mystery bags for each student or group of students working together:

  (*a*) 3 small paper bags labeled "X," "Y," and "Z"

  (*b*) 50 chips—30 red and 20 blue—for each bag

  (*c*) 15 stars (or other stickers) for each bag

pp. 84–89

Discussion

This activity presents students with a scenario about dogs that have just finished an obedience course at an establishment called Abby's Kennels. Of 50 dogs enrolled in the five-session course, 30 dogs were large (as measured by weight), and 20 dogs were small. A total of 15 dogs passed the course.

The activity lets students explore ways of thinking about the probability of two events—"selecting a dog of a particular size" (large or small) and "selecting a dog with a particular course result" (passed or did not pass)—occurring in the selection of a single dog from the population of 50 dogs that were enrolled in the obedience course at Abby's Kennels. The students use simulation, relative frequencies, and conditional probabilities to investigate the probabilities of selecting a dog of a particular size with particular course results.

The simulation requires three "mystery bags" that you will need to prepare in advance for each student or small group of students who will be working together, depending on how you decide to have students do the activity. Discovering the composition of the mystery bags helps students develop the idea of independence.

To make each set of mystery bags, label three small opaque bags "X," "Y," and "Z," and put 50 chips in each—30 red chips to represent the large dogs and 20 blue chips to represent the small dogs in the course at Abby's Kennels. To complete the bags—

- place a star (or other sticker) on any 15 red chips in bag X;
- place a star (or other sticker) on 9 red chips and 6 blue chips in bag Y;
- place a star (or other sticker) on 15 blue chips in bag Z.

The stars or stickers will represent the dogs that passed the obedience course.

Whether you have your students work independently or in groups, you should have each student collect data individually, as the activity pages direct, and record the data in the appropriate tables and charts. (Having the students work in small groups will reduce the number of

mystery bags that you will need and will also facilitate the students' collection of data.)

In the activity, students select chips to simulate selecting dogs at random from the 50 dogs that completed the obedience course at Abby's Kennels. After simulating the selection of a dog, the students record its size (large or small) and its obedience course result (passed or did not pass). The scenario supplies the numbers of small and large dogs, as well as the total number of dogs that passed the obedience course. Other characteristics of the group of dogs, such as the number of large dogs that passed the course, are not known. (Table 3.1 shows the data from the scenario entered in a two-way table such as students work with in the activity.)

Table 3.1
Obedience Course Results for Large and Small Dogs at Abby's Kennels

	Passed the Course	Did Not Pass the Course	Total
Large dogs			30
Small dogs			20
Total	15	35	50

As students select chips from each bag, the activity guides them in using relative frequencies to make conjectures about the make-up of each bag. Students are encouraged to articulate their observations about their data, which they summarize in tables (figure 3.1 shows a sample).

Fig. **3.1.**

A sample activity table for summarizing descriptors of dogs represented by chips selected from a mystery bag

Descriptors of Dogs Represented by Chips Selected from Bag Y			
Selection Number	Large Dog (Red Chip)	Small Dog (Blue Chip)	Dog That Passed the Obedience Course (Chip with Star)
1			
2			
3			
4			
5			
6			
7			
8			
9			
10			

Summaries that indicate that all the dogs that passed the obedience course are large (bag X), or that none of the dogs that passed the obedience course is large (bag Z), indicate events that are not independent. That is, for bag X, the first event "selecting a large dog" affects—in this case, *increases*—the likelihood of the second event "selecting a dog that passed the obedience course." This likelihood—15/30, or 1/2—is not the same as the likelihood of selecting a dog that passed the obedience course if the first event happened to be "selecting a small dog." For bag X, *this* first event would *decrease* the likelihood of the second event "selecting a dog that passed the obedience course" to 0/20, or 0.

When students investigate bag Y, they should begin to offer statements that indicate their recognition that the events involving the size of a dog and its obedience course results are independent. They should discover that the likelihood of selecting a dog that passed the obedience course is "not noticeably different" for large or small dogs. That is, the likelihood of the event "selecting a dog that passed the obedience course" does not depend on the prior occurrence of the event "selecting a large [or a small] dog."

For bag Y, the exact proportion for selecting a chip that represents a dog that passed the course, given the occurrence of the event "selecting a large dog," is 9/30, or 3/10. This proportion is equal to the proportion for selecting a chip that represents a dog that passed the course, given the occurrence of the event "selecting a small dog" (6/20, or 3/10). The equality of these proportions indicates that the event "selecting a dog that passed the course" and the event "selecting a dog of a particular size" are independent. This proportion, 3/10, is thus also equal to the proportion for selecting a dog that passed the course without regard to size: 15/50, or 3/10.

Bag Y presents students with the activity's central challenge. It is unlikely that the data that they collect from this bag will demonstrate the exact proportions for selecting a dog that is large and that has passed the obedience course. Students should, however, observe that they are obtaining similar ratios for both large and small dogs that passed or did not pass the course. Question 10 formally presents the composition of the bag to the students through a two-way table.

The activity, which began with the task of estimating probabilities from relative frequencies, concludes with a more formal consideration of conditional probabilities and independence. Conditional probability is explained with an example that calls on students to consider the likelihood of selecting a dog that passed the obedience course *given that* the dog (selected from bag Y) is large. Students are told that this probability is represented symbolically as $P(A \mid B)$, where, in the example, A stands for "selecting a dog that passed the course," and B stands for "selecting a large dog."

Questions 13 and 14 ask the students to use the data that they tabulated for bag Y to determine the probability that a randomly selected dog passed the course, given the size of the dog. Deriving conditional probabilities from a two-way table provides the students with a mechanism for determining whether or not the events are independent. According to the definition of independence supplied to the students in question 12, two events A and B are considered *independent* if the probability of both A and B occurring in a single selection from a population is the product of the probability of the first event times the probability of the second event.

This relationship is represented symbolically as $P(A \cap B) = P(A) \cdot P(B)$. If A and B are independent events, then $P(A \mid B) = P(A)$. This result can be derived by applying the multiplication principle to substitute $P(A) \cdot P(B)$ for $P(A \cap B)$ in the statement of conditional probabilities and then simplifying, as shown in figure 3.2.

The activity prompts students to think about what conditional probabilities tell them about the independence of events and to consider what independence means. In the data that students gather on the dogs

If all the dogs that passed the obedience course are large, or if none of the dogs that passed the obedience course is large, then the events "selecting a dog that is large" and "selecting a dog that passed the course" are not independent.

If $P(A)$ represents the probability that event A will occur and $P(B)$ represents the probability that event B will occur, then the conditional probability, $P(A|B)$, which denotes the probability of event A given event B, is defined in the following way:

$$P(A \mid B) = \frac{P(A \text{ and } B)}{P(B)} = \frac{P(A \cap B)}{P(B)}.$$

Recall from chapter 2 that for *independent* events A and B, P(A and B) is given by the multiplication principle: $P(A \cap B) = P(A) \cdot P(B)$.

enrolled in obedience training at Abby's Kennels, independence would mean that the probability of selecting a dog that passed the course (event A) from the population of large dogs (given event B) would be the same as the probability of selecting a dog that passed the obedience course from the total population of dogs with no condition given about the dog's size.

Fig. **3.2.**

Derivation of $P(A \mid B) = P(A)$ for independent events

If A and B are independent events, then the probability of A, given the occurrence of B, is equal to the probability of A:

$$P(A \mid B) = \frac{P(A \cap B)}{P(B)}$$ Statement of conditional probabilities

$$P(A \cap B) = P(A) \cdot P(B)$$ Multiplication principle for independent events

$$P(A \mid B) = \frac{P(A) \cdot P(B)}{P(B)}$$ Substitution

$$\frac{P(A) \cdot P(B)}{P(B)} = P(A)$$ Simplification

$$\therefore P(A \mid B) = P(A)$$ Substitution

Students use the specific values organized in the two-way table for bag Y to summarize the independence of the course results and the sizes of the dogs. For example, if A, the event "selecting a dog that passed the course," and B, the event "selecting a large dog," are independent, then the multiplication principle may be used to demonstrate that $P(A \cap B)$ equals $P(A) \bullet P(B)$. In addition, students may use the two-way table to demonstrate that each conditional probability is equal to the probability of selecting a dog that passed the course from the total population of 50 dogs. This information helps them answer concluding questions about how they would expect a trainer at Abby's Kennels to respond if asked whether dogs of different sizes could be expected to have different results in an obedience training course.

The next activity, Independent or Not Independent? presents the results of a high school survey on asthma and cigarette smoke. The activity gives students an opportunity to examine a population in which two events are not independent.

Additional lessons that develop ideas about compound events have been reprinted by permission (in both teacher and student editions) from Hopfensperger, Kranendonk, and Scheaffer (1999) on the accompanying CD-ROM.

Independent or
Not Independent?

Goal

- Use conditional probabilities to understand when two events are
  not independent

Materials and Equipment

- A copy of the activity pages for each student

pp. 90–93

Discussion

As students begin to understand the meaning of independence, they
can appreciate an important aspect of the process involved in many
research projects. Independent or not independent—that is the question! The activity Independent or Not Independent? focuses on a scenario about a research project on asthma and cigarette smoke under-
taken at a fictitious high school. Students at South High School
collected data by means of an all-school survey and analyzed them to
determine whether or not the events "selecting a South High School
student with asthma" and "selecting a South High School student living
in a household with one or more smokers" were independent.

In working through this activity, your students will again use the
process of organizing data in a two-way table to help them determine
whether or not two events are independent. Since the data presented in
the table give a summary of an entire population, the students do not
need to estimate probabilities empirically, with relative frequencies, but
can determine them analytically, by evaluating possible outcomes.

Pursuing ideas from the activity about the dogs at Abby's Kennels,
this activity provides the students with another scenario that illustrates
the usefulness of analyzing conditional probabilities to determine
whether or not events are independent. As students work with the
South High School scenario, their consideration of the events "selecting an asthmatic student" and "selecting a student who lives in a household with one or more smokers" reinforces their understanding of the
process of organizing data and analyzing conditional probabilities. This
time the process shows them that the events are not independent.

It is important to note that numerous examples of research studies
exist that are similar to this project except that they rely on data from a
sample instead of an entire population. If the students at South High
School had collected data from a sample of South High students instead
of from the total population of students at the school, then the questions that involve probability in the activity could have been expanded
to include questions that involved inference, as well.

Deciding whether or not events are independent becomes more
complex when inference from a sample to a larger population comes
into play. Appropriate analysis of independence then requires the use of
statistical methods. Because the activity Independent or Not Independent? presents data gathered from the total student population at South

Navigating through Data
Analysis in Grades 9–12
*(Burrill et al. 2003) offers
ways to present statistical
methods to high school
students.*

High School rather than from a sample of the students at the school, drawing conclusions about the independence of events does not require the specialized, more sophisticated methods of data analysis.

In the activity, students arrange the data about asthma and cigarette smoke in a two-way table, as shown in table 3.2. The activity then guides them in imagining that the table has been "pulled apart" into rows and that they have only separate pieces (questions 4 and 5). This process helps them focus on the conditional probabilities shown by the data in each row (questions 6 and 7).

Table 3.2
Household Composition (with or without Smokers) of Asthmatic and Nonasthmatic Students at South High School

	Households with One or More Smokers	Households without Smokers	Total
Asthmatic students	113	69	182
Nonasthmatic students	282	473	755
Total	395	542	937

Having students rearrange these data in a second two-way table that switches the rows and columns from the first table can enrich this activity. If students continue to show an interest in the data on asthma and smokers in households, they can be presented with the second two-way table, which is shown here as table 3.3.

Table 3.3
Table 3.2 with Rows and Columns Reversed

	Asthmatic Students	Nonasthmatic Students	Total
Households with one or more smokers	113	282	395
Households without smokers	69	473	542
Total	182	755	937

Using the model of the "pulled apart" table in the activity pages and the questions posed there about the conditional probabilities shown by the rows, ask your students about the conditional probabilities that they could derive from this rearranged table. As students discuss the connections and conditional probabilities, the following summaries should emerge:

- The probability that a student selected at random has asthma when the selection is made from those students who live in a household with one or more smokers is 113/395, or about 28.6 percent.
- The probability that a student selected at random has asthma when the selection is made from those students who live in households *without* smokers is 69/542, or about 12.7 percent.

The inequality of these conditional probabilities indicates that having asthma and living in a household with one or more smokers are not independent events. If they were, the probabilities would be the same. Working with conditional probabilities based on data in the rearranged table should bring the students to the same conclusion that their work in the activity did—that the events are not independent.

It is important to emphasize to students that this result does not "prove" that smoking causes asthma but only that the two events are not independent in the population studied—that is, the students at South High School. A discussion of research that is directed at demonstrating cause and effect can be an extension of this type of investigation. For example, students might investigate the history of studies on smoking and cancer.

Conclusion

This chapter has examined the probability of the occurrence of one event, given the occurrence of another event. Working with and understanding conditional probabilities gives students a powerful insight into the independence or nonindependence of events. The activities in this chapter provide models for using numerous studies to investigate the connections around us. As students begin to understand these ideas, their abilities to analyze the larger picture and make sense of society and the world advance.

NAVIGATING *through* PROBABILITY

Chapter 4
Probability Models and Distributions

A benefit of solving problems by applying probability theory is that beautiful mathematical patterns, both numerical and graphical, often emerge. These patterns define entire classes of probability problems that have similar structures. Probability models can be used to solve a variety of problems that fall into these classes, which span a wide range of contexts and situations.

The principal ideas in this chapter are the concepts of a *probability distribution* and a *random variable*. *Principles and Standards for School Mathematics* (NCTM 2000, p. 324) suggests that students in grades 9–12 should—

- Understand the concepts of sample space and probability distribution and construct sample spaces and probability distributions in simple cases;
- Use simulations to construct empirical probability distributions.

Among the most common of all probability situations, and the most widely applicable, are those that can be modeled by the *binomial probability distribution* or the *geometric probability distribution*.

Situations Modeled by Binomial Experiments

Consider these scenarios and questions:

- A woman came to trial in a controversial case involving domestic violence. When prospective jurors were called to the twelve-member jury panel, the initial panel consisted of 11 men and 1 woman.

Let us assume a simplified model in which the ratio of men to women in a jury pool is one to one and remains constant throughout the jury selection process. How likely would this defendant be to draw an initial panel of 11 men and 1 woman in the selection of a jury for her trial?

- The manufacturer of M&M's claims that yellow M&M's compose 20 percent of its mixture and that its production process creates a random mixing of colors in the bags prepared for sale. What then would be the probability of buying a bag of 30 M&M's with no yellows?

- Many people believe that if they toss 10 fair coins, their chance of getting 5 heads is quite good. If you tossed 10 fair coins, what would be the probability that you would get exactly 5 heads? If you tossed the 10 coins 100 times and recorded the number of heads each time, what would a frequency distribution of the number of heads look like?

- In 1987, Major League baseball player Paul Molitor of the Milwaukee Brewers batted nearly .400 for most of the season. Assuming that Molitor maintained a constant .400 batting average, calculate the probability that he would get at least one hit in three times at bat. How about at least one hit in four at-bats? What would be his chance of getting three hits in three at-bats? Of getting four hits in four at-bats?

We can extend this last scenario to ask other questions involving probability:

- Paul Molitor also enjoyed quite a long hitting streak in the 1987 baseball season. During one stretch of 39 consecutive games, he got at least one hit in every game. What would be the probability that a hypothetical player whose batting average remained constant at .400 and who came to bat three times in every game would get at least one hit in each of 39 games in a row? What if the player came to bat four times in every game?

We can simplify and mathematize these questions hypothetically so that they all have four essential characteristics:

1. They involve a sequence of one or more repeated trials.
2. Each trial has two (and only two) possible outcomes.
3. The trials are independent of one another.
4. The probabilities of the two outcomes are the same in every trial.

Probability questions with these characteristics are called binomial probability problems because they involve two, and only two, outcomes.

For example, each juror selected is either a man or a woman. If we imagine that the ratio of men to women in a pool of prospective jurors is one to one and remains constant throughout the jury selection process, men and women will both have a .5 probability of being chosen. In this hypothetical situation, previous choices of jurors would not change the probability of a man or woman being called in subsequent choices; choices of jurors would be independent events. Likewise, each candy drawn from a bag of M&M's would be either yellow, with a probability given by the manufacturer as .20, or not yellow, with a probability of .80. In the problem involving the tossing of 10 fair coins, each outcome—heads or tails—has a probability of .5 on each try.

For the scenarios based on Paul Molitor's batting success in 1987, a simplified model can be created if one assumes that only the outcome "hit" or "not a hit" (or "no hit") is possible on each trial and that the player would have a probability of .4 of getting a hit every time he came to bat. The real baseball situation is much more complicated, since more than two outcomes are possible on each try, and the repeated trials are not independent. (The next chapter will take another look at Paul Molitor's impressive 39-game hitting streak and will examine the likelihood that a hypothetical player with a batting average like Molitor's would accomplish such a feat.)

Random Variables

The simplified batting model just discussed serves as the basis for this chapter's first activity, What's the Probability of a Hit? In this activity, students consider the binomial outcomes "hit" and "not a hit" (or "no hit") to explore the probability that a baseball player who maintained a constant batting average of .400 would get at least two hits in three at-bats. In this investigation, students informally encounter the notion of *random variable*.

Students can use the Binomial Distribution Simulator applet on the CD-ROM to gather simulated data to investigate the probability that a baseball player with a constant batting average of .400 will get at least two hits in three at-bats.

What's the Probability
of a Hit?

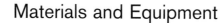

Goals

- Explore a binomial distribution problem
- Approach a binomial probability problem through an of investigation of relative frequencies as well as through an analysis of outcomes, and compare the two approaches
- Use binomial distribution simulation software to confirm calculations of theoretical probabilities for a binomial distribution problem

Materials and Equipment

pp. 94–97

- A copy of the activity pages for each student
- Materials for simulations—for example, random number tables, graphing calculators with a random number function (or other software capable of generating random numbers, such as the Random Number Generator applet), or
- Binomial distribution simulation software, such as the Binomial Distribution Simulator applet

Discussion

Every binomial probability situation involves a certain number n ($n \geq 1$) of independent, repeated trials. Two outcomes are possible on any single trial, with probabilities p and q, where $p + q = 1$. In the activity What's the Probability of a Hit? $p = .4$ ("a hit"), $q = .6$ ("not a hit"), and $n = 3$, because there are three times at bat. A hit constitutes a "success," and students are interested in the number of successes in three at-bats. At a more general level, we can say that the students are interested in the number of successes in a sequence of n trials and in the probability of various numbers of successes occurring in sequences of n trials.

If X stands for "the number of hits in three at-bats," the values of X could be 0, 1, 2, or 3, depending on the number of hits that the player succeeded in getting in three at-bats. X is a *random variable*, and statisticians are typically interested in the probabilities of all the values of a random variable. The notation $P(X = 1)$ stands for "the probability that the random variable X takes on the value 1."

In the example of the baseball player in the activity, let H represent "hit" and N represent "not a hit," or "no hit." If any or all of the outcomes with exactly one hit (HNN, NHN, NNH) occur, $X = 1$. Using the addition and multiplication principles, $P(X = 1) = P(\text{HNN}) + P(\text{NHN}) + P(\text{NNH}) = [(.4) \cdot (.6) \cdot (.6)] + [(.6) \cdot (.4) \cdot (.6)] + [(.6) \cdot (.6) \cdot (.4)] = .144 + .144 + .144 = .432.$

The probabilities that $X = 2$, 3, and 0 (2 hits, 3 hits, and 0 hits in three at-bats) can be found in the same way. Using the sample space and the addition and multiplication principles gives the following:

$P(X = 2) = [P(\text{HHN}) + P(\text{NHH}) + P(\text{HNH})] = 3 \cdot [(.4)^2 \cdot .6] = .288;$
$P(X = 3) = P(\text{HHH}) = (.4)^3 = .064;$
$P(X = 0) = P(\text{NNN}) = (.6)^3 = .216.$

The possible values of the random variable and the probabilities associated with these values constitute the *probability distribution* for the random variable *X*. Note that the sum of all the probabilities in a distribution is 1. In the case of the baseball player,

$P(X = 0) + P(X = 1) + P(X = 2) + P(X = 3) = .216 + .432 + .288 + .064 = 1.$

> The sum of the probabilities of all the values of a random variable is always equal to 1.

Number of Outcomes in a Binomial Distribution

The total number of outcomes for a binomial experiment depends on the number, *n*, of repeated trials. For example, there are two outcomes for each at-bat in the batter problem—a hit (H) and no hit (N). As a result, for two at-bats, there are 2 • 2, or 4, outcomes: {HH, HN, NH, NN}. There are 2 • 2 • 2, or 8, possible outcomes for three at-bats, as students discover in the activity What's the Probability of a Hit? In general, if there are *n* repeated trials in a binomial experiment, there are $2 \cdot 2 \cdot \ldots \cdot 2$, or 2^n, outcomes in the sample space associated with a binomial distribution.

In the late nineteenth century, Sir Francis Galton built his famous quincunx machine, which provided a visual model of the distribution of binomial outcomes in repeated trials (see fig. 4.1). Steel marbles were funneled into a slot at the top of the machine and dropped through it. As they descended, they hit successive rows of evenly spaced pegs, which were offset from one another as shown.

At each peg, the balls could bounce randomly either left or right, making two outcomes possible. Thus, Galton created a binomial machine, which displayed the results of repeated independent trials and represented the two outcomes of each trial by the branching of bouncing balls at each peg. Galton could alter the probabilities that the marbles would branch one way or the other at each peg by tilting his machine to one side or the other.

The accompanying CD-ROM includes several binomial activities developed by Shaughnessy and Arcidiacono (1993) for a checker game board that is similar to Galton's quincunx. These activities can help students make the connection between the number of branching paths that can bring a ball to a given peg in Galton's quincunx machine, or a checker to a given square in a checkerboard, and the probability that the dropping ball, or the moving checker, ends up in that particular place.

The activities can also help students connect the number of possible paths with the numbers that appear in the rows of Pascal's triangle. The first few rows of Pascal's triangle are shown in figure 4.2. The numerals (except 1 in the 0th row) represent the number of paths that dropped balls can traverse to reach corresponding pegs.

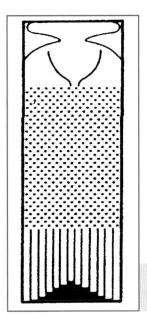

See Hilsenrath and Field (1983) on the CD-ROM for a discussion of a computer program that simulates the dropping of balls through rows of pegs in the Galton quincunx.

Fig. **4.1.**

The Galton quincunx

Fig. **4.2.**

Pascal's triangle

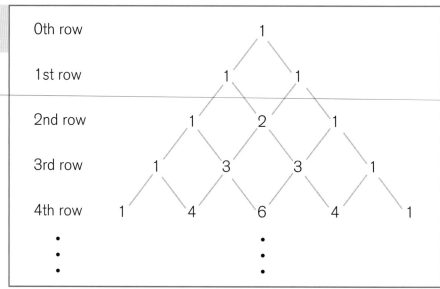

The first peg that a marble dropped in Galton's quincunx hits can be thought of as corresponding to 1 in the zeroth row of Pascal's triangle. The marble then bounces left or right. To travel to a peg corresponding to 2 in the triangle, the marble has two possible paths. To travel to a peg corresponding to either 3 in the triangle, it has three possible paths, and so on.

Students have another, more explicit opportunity to investigate a random variable X and to examine the binomial distribution of the probabilities that are associated with its values in the next activity, How Likely Is That Jury? The discussion of this activity considers Pascal's triangle again and elaborates on its usefulness in calculating probabilities in repeated trials with binomial outcomes.

How Likely Is That Jury?

Goals

- Explore a binomial distribution problem
- Approach a binomial probability problem through an investigation of relative frequencies as well as through an analysis of outcomes, and compare the two approaches
- Use binomial distribution simulation software to confirm theoretical probability calculations for a binomial distribution problem

Materials and Equipment

- A copy of the activity pages for each student
- Materials for simulations—for example, random number tables, graphing calculators with a random number function (or other software capable of generating random numbers, such as the Random Number Generator applet), or
- Binomial distribution simulation software, such as the Binomial Distribution Simulator applet

Discussion

The activity How Likely Is That Jury? raises the question posed in the first scenario presented in this chapter: How likely is it that 11 men and 1 woman would be called initially to a jury panel from a pool of prospective jurors consisting of equal numbers of men and women? The students are asked to assume a simplified situation, in which the ratio of men to women in the jury pool remains one to one throughout. As in the previous activity, students analyze theoretical outcomes and compare them with empirical relative frequencies, derived this time from simulations of jury panels.

This activity provides students and teachers with an excellent opportunity for an extension that can take students beyond the activity to a more general investigation. They can use their understanding of a random variable and a binomial distribution to explore the question "Which compositions of men and women are likely on a twelve-member jury, and which are unlikely?"

Since in this scenario half of all potential jurors are men and half are women, most juries should fall in a range between panels made up of three men and nine women and panels made up of nine men and three women. Randomly selected juries that have ten or more members of one gender are unlikely events, as students should discover in doing the simulation in How Likely Is That Jury? Randomly selected juries with an 11 to 1 ratio are quite rare.

How Likely Is That Jury? presents a binomial probability problem in which the two outcomes, man and woman, or M and W, both have a probability of .5 of occurring each time a prospective juror is called, and there can be $n = 0, 1, 2, …, 12$ women on a jury. In general, if a binomial probability problem has probabilities p and q for the two outcomes, where $p + q = 1$, and if X is the random variable that takes on values $0, 1, 2, …, n$, for the number of "successes" in n trials, then the

pp. 98–99

Students can use the Binomial Distribution Simulator applet on the CD to gather simulated data to investigate the likelihood of calling 11 or 12 men to a 12-member jury panel in the activity How Likely Is That Jury?

By running repeated simulations on the Binomial Probability Simulator on the CD-ROM, or Prob Sim (Konold and Craig 1992; for Macintosh; available on the CD-ROM by permission), students can determine jury compositions that account for most juries—say, around 90 to 95 percent of them.

The number of unordered subsets of size *r* from a set of *n* objects is the number of combinations of *n* things taken *r* at a time. This number can be expressed as *C*(*n*, *r*) and can be found with the formula

$$C(n,r) = \frac{n!}{(n-r)!\,r!}$$

probability distribution for *X* can be found as follows:

For $0 \le r \le n$,

$$P(X = r) = C(n, r) \cdot p^r \cdot q^{(n-r)},$$

where *C*(*n*, *r*) is the coefficient of the term p^r in the expansion of the binomial $(p + q)^n$.

C(*n*, *r*) is also the number of unordered subsets, or combinations, of size *r* that can be formed from a set of *n* objects. Furthermore, *C*(*n*, *r*) is the (*r* + 1)st entry in the *n*th row of Pascal's triangle. Many such mathematical connections arise in the binomial distribution.

"Wait Until" Probability Problems: The Geometric Distribution

Some of the most interesting probability problems involve repeated trials with binomial outcomes and probe "streaks" of occurrences of a particular outcome. Or they investigate how long we might expect to "wait until" a particular outcome occurs. For example—

- Assume that jurors are randomly chosen from a pool with a constant one-to-one ratio of men to women. What is the probability that you would have to "wait until" the fifth juror was selected before a woman was called? What is the probability that you would have to wait until the tenth juror was selected?

- Suppose that a baseball player's batting average remained a constant .400. What is the probability that this player would have a streak of 10 consecutive games in which she made at least one hit in every game (assuming that she came to bat three times in each game and that the only outcomes of each at-bat are a hit or no hit).

- The manufacturer of M&M's claims that yellow candies make up 20 percent of its mixture. Assume that the production process creates a random mixing of colors in bags of M&M's prepared for sale. Suppose that you were in an M&M's factory and you began blindly selecting candies from a huge vat that was constantly refilled with candies of the same colors as those that you had selected. What is the probability that you would have to "wait until" your fifth selection before you got a yellow one? What is the probability that you would have to wait until your tenth selection?

Each of these questions involves a situation that is essentially binomial, with only two outcomes for each trial, as well as a sequence of independent trials. However, this time the question asks about the probability of a "streak" of occurrences of a certain outcome, or a different kind of "streak"—a stretch of "waiting until" a certain outcome occurs in repeated trials.

The next activity, Consecutive Hits—Consecutively Hitless, allows your students to explore a problem of this type. The students again examine the scenario involving the baseball player with a constant batting average of .400. This time, they investigate the probability that the player would go hitless until the fourth at-bat or, conversely, would get a hit in each of the first three at-bats and then go hitless on the fourth try. This activity gives students an opportunity to examine probabilities that in repeated trials decrease like a geometric sequence.

Many interesting probability problems involve "wait until" questions of the form "How many repeated trials *would you expect* until you first observed a particular outcome?" For example, on average—

- How many jurors *would you expect* to be selected before a woman was called to a 12-member panel?

- In how many consecutive games *would you expect* a .400 hitter to get at least one hit if she came to bat three times in every game?

- How many candies *would you expect* to pull before you get the first yellow candy?

These types of questions about an *expected value* are considered in chapter 5.

Consecutive Hits—
Consecutively Hitless

Goals

- Explore a geometric distribution problem

- Approach a binomial probability problem through an investigation of relative frequencies as well as through an analysis of outcomes, and compare the two approaches

- Use geometric distribution simulation software to confirm calculations of theoretical probabilities for a geometric distribution problem

Materials and Equipment

- A copy of the activity pages for each student

- Materials for simulations—for example, random number tables, graphing calculators with a random number function (or other software capable of generating random numbers, such as the Random Number Generator applet), or

- Geometric probability simulation software, such as the Geometric Distribution Simulator applet

Discussion

The tree diagram in figure 4.3 shows the probabilities associated with the sequences of outcomes for three at-bats taken by the hypothetical player with the constant batting average of .400. All "wait until" contexts lead to a probability distribution that descends like a geometric sequence. For example, assuming that men and women were equally likely to be chosen for a jury from a jury pool with a constant one-to-one ratio of men to women, you could model the process of choosing jurors randomly until a woman appeared on the panel by flipping a coin until you obtained a head (representing a woman juror). The probability that a head would appear on the first toss is one-half—that is, $P(H) = .5$. The probability that you would need to wait until the second toss for a head to appear—that is, $P(TH)$, since your first toss would have been a tail—is $(.5) \cdot (.5)$, or .25.

In a similar fashion, you could use the multiplication principle to calculate the probability that the first head (representing the first woman juror) appeared on your third toss—$P(TTH) = (.5) \cdot (.5) \cdot (.5)$ $= .125$—or on the fourth toss—$P(TTTH) = (.5)^4 = .0625$. In general, the probability that the first head (a woman juror) would appear on the nth toss is $(.5)^n$. The shape of this distribution is shown in figure 4.4. Each bar is half as tall as the preceding bar, thus illustrating the term *geometric distribution*, which denotes a distribution of probabilities that descend in the manner of a geometric sequence.

pp. 100–101

Students can use the Geometric Distribution Simulator applet on the CD-ROM to examine the declining probabilities of strings of outcomes from repeated trials.

Fig. **4.3.**

A tree diagram of the probabilities of the batting sequences for three at-bats for a player with a constant batting average of .400 (H indicates a hit, and N indicates no hit)

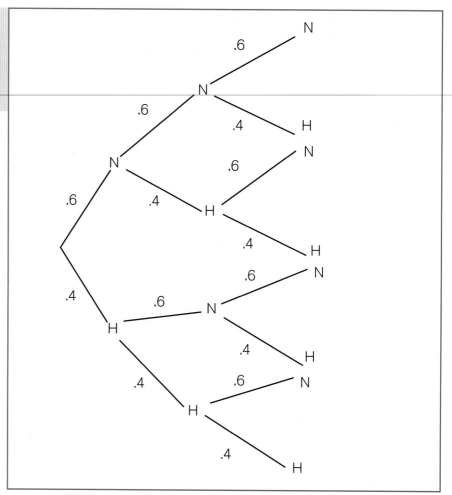

All the activities in this chapter direct students to run 50 trials with random numbers or the applets or other probability distribution software. There is nothing special about 50 trials, and you may wish to have your students work with larger numbers of repetitions or pool data to confirm the results of larger numbers of trials.

Fig. **4.4.**

The probability that the first head would appear on the *n*th toss of a coin if $1 \leq n \leq 4$

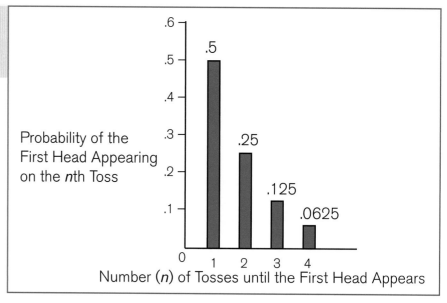

Probability of the First Head Appearing on the *n*th Toss

Conclusion

This chapter has investigated applications of two of the most useful probability distributions—the binomial distribution and the geometric distribution. There are many other probability distributions, including the chi-square distribution, the normal distribution, and the Poisson distribution. Students should gather actual data and conduct simulations before or along with their use of formulas to calculate probabilities directly. These processes of collecting data are important to the development of the students' intuitions about the likelihoods of various outcomes and the shapes of the graphs of probability distributions. This philosophy stands behind the activities in this chapter.

NAVIGATING *through* PROBABILITY

Chapter 5
Expected Value

"All students should … compute and interpret the expected value of random variables in simple cases."
(NCTM 2000, p. 324)

The probability distribution for a random variable can be used to predict the average value in the long run, or the *expected value*, of the random variable. The concept of expected value is widely used in decision making. For example, life insurance companies use expected-value calculations to determine premiums that they can expect to attract customers while ensuring a profit. Airlines use the number of passengers who can be expected to be "no-shows" to decide by how many seats to overbook flights so that they will have a good chance of being full. Testing agencies design scoring schemes that take account of the number of questions that students can be expected to answer correctly by guessing.

Principles and Standards for School Mathematics (NCTM 2000) recommends that all students in grades 9–12 be able to "compute and interpret the expected value of random variables in simple cases" (p. 324). The activities in this chapter ask students to use simulated data to develop their intuitions and confirm their computations of expected value. As students discuss the activities, they should realize that the expected value—

* *does not* provide information about the outcome of an individual trial;
* *does* provide information about the average value of the outcome in the long run, over many trials.

Students should work on the chapter's three activities in pairs or small groups, especially when they are designing or conducting simulations.

The first activity, One-Girl Family Planning, introduces students to the concept and definition of expected value. This activity complements and extends the activity One-Boy Family Planning in chapter 1.

One-Girl Family Planning

Goals

- Use simulated data and a geometric probability distribution to investigate an expected value
- Develop the concept and definition of expected value
- Compare an expected value obtained with relative frequencies to an expected value obtained with theoretical probabilities

Materials and Equipment

pp. 102–4

- A copy of the activity pages for each student (or pair of students)
- Students' data from table 2 of One-Boy Family Planning (p. 74)
- Materials for simulations—for example, cards, dice, random number tables, graphing calculators with a random number function (or other software capable of generating random numbers, such as the Random Number Generator applet), or
- Geometric probability simulation software, such as the Geometric Distribution Simulator applet

Discussion

In chapter 1, the activity One-Boy Family Planning lets students explore the sizes of sibling groups that would theoretically result under a one-boy policy of family planning. The activity gives students some insight into the average number of children that families could be expected to have in a country that adopted such a policy.

The activity One-Girl Family Planning turns the scenario, asking students to consider a hypothetical country in which girls have a higher status than boys. The country in this new situation adopts a one-girl policy to limit population growth. The policy allows couples to have children until they have a girl, but then they cannot have any more children. Students can work individually or in pairs and are asked to assume that all couples capable of having children will continue to do so until they produce a girl.

The activity pages present simulated data that students in another class gathered on the sizes of sibling groups under the policy. Your students can work from these data, or they can use data of their own. If your students previously completed the activity One-Boy Family Planning, they can use the simulated data that they recorded in table 2 (page 74), since the probabilities of male and female births are close enough to .5 to be treated as equal. Alternatively, you can have your students conduct a new simulation to collect data for One-Girl Family Planning.

Using data from simulations to calculate the mean number of children in sibling groups can help students formulate the definition of expected value. To see how the definition develops from this computation, consider the data in table 5.1. These 500 sibling groups simulated by students in another class are also shown on the first activity page (p. 102) for "One-Girl Family Planning." None of these simulated sibling groups has more than nine children.

Table 5.1
Observed Frequencies of Different-Sized Simulated Sibling Groups under a One-Girl Policy of Family Planning (Data Gathered in Another Class)

Number of children in a sibling group	1	2	3	4	5	6	7	8	9	Total
Observed frequency	242	128	59	32	24	8	3	2	2	500

The mean number, $\bar{x}$, of children from these 500 sibling groups can be calculated as follows:

$$\bar{x} = \frac{242 \cdot 1 + 128 \cdot 2 + 59 \cdot 3 + 32 \cdot 4 + 24 \cdot 5 + 8 \cdot 6 + 3 \cdot 7 + 2 \cdot 8 + 2 \cdot 9}{500}$$

$$= 1\left(\frac{242}{500}\right) + 2\left(\frac{128}{500}\right) + 3\left(\frac{59}{500}\right) + \ldots + 9\left(\frac{2}{500}\right)$$

$$\approx 2.1$$

Students can see the definition of expected value developing in the second row of the calculation. The numbers 1, 2, ..., 9 are simply the numbers of children, or the values of the random variable, that occurred in the simulated sibling groups. Note that there could have been additional outcomes, and in fact families with more than 9 children would be expected to occur if more trials were performed. The fractions 242/500, 128/500, ..., 2/500 are the relative frequencies, or the empirical probabilities, resulting from the simulation. One way to calculate the mean number of children from the 500 simulated sibling groups is to multiply each outcome by its relative frequency and add the products.

This procedure can be used again, this time with theoretical probabilities from the problem's geometric distribution, to compute the expected mean number of children in a very large number of sibling groups. Teachers should encourage students to use different large numbers of sibling groups—for example, 500, 1000, or 10 000. Students should share the results of their calculations so that they understand clearly that expected value is independent of the number of trials.

To guide students in a formulation of the definition of expected value, one student could explain the steps in his or her computations. For example, suppose a student has based the computation on 1000 sibling groups. Most likely the student will first multiply each theoretical probability (1/2, 1/4, 1/8, etc.) by 1000 to obtain the expected frequency for sibling groups of each size. Then the student would probably multiply each frequency and corresponding number of children in the simulated sibling group before summing the products to obtain the total number of children. The final step would be to divide by 1000 to calculate the mean number of children per family. Figure 5.1 shows the steps in this process.

At the completion of this activity, students should realize that their first computation, which was based on simulated data, provides them with the average number of children in some number of simulated sibling groups, and their second computation, which was based on

Fig. **5.1.**

Theoretical probabilities used to calculate
the expected mean number of children per
sibling group in 1000 sibling groups under
a one-girl policy

Group size	Theoretical probability × 1000 sibling groups = Number of groups
1	1/2 × 1000 = 500
2	1/4 × 1000 = 250
3	1/8 × 1000 = 125
4	1/16 × 1000 = 62.5 ≈ 63
5	1/32 × 1000 = 31.25 ≈ 31
6	1/64 × 1000 = 15.625 ≈ 16
7	1/128 × 1000 = 7.813 ≈ 8
8	1/256 × 1000 = 3.906 ≈ 4
9	1/512 × 1000 = 1.953 ≈ 2
10	1/1024 × 1000 = 0.977 ≈ 1

And so on …

Group size	Number of groups × Group size = Number of children
1	500 × 1 = 500
2	250 × 2 = 500
3	125 × 3 = 375
4	62.5 × 4 = 250
5	31.25 × 5 = 156.25 ≈ 156
6	15.625 × 6 = 93.75 ≈ 94
7	7.813 × 7 ≈ 54.69 ≈ 55
8	3.906 × 8 ≈ 31.25 ≈ 31
9	1.953 × 9 ≈ 17.58 ≈ 18
10	0.977 × 10 = 9.77 ≈ 10

And so on …

Total number of children in 1000 sibling groups:
500 + 500 + 375 + 250 + 156 + 94 + 55 +31
$$+ 18 + 10 + \ldots \approx 2000$$
Mean number of children per sibling group
(or Total number of children ÷ Total number of sibling groups):
(approximately 2000) ÷ 1000 ≈ 2,
or, on average, 2 children per sibling group
Note: Even considering the rounding of numbers, we can see that
the total is approximately 2000.

As an extra activity, an advanced class could show that a random variable X with a geometric distribution and a probability of success p has as expected value of 1/p.

theoretical probabilities, provides them with the average number of children that would be *expected* in a large number of theoretical sibling groups. Since the second average is based entirely on what probability leads us to expect to happen in the long run, it is called the *expected value* of the random variable:

$$\text{Expected value of } X = E(X) = \Sigma x_i P(x_i),$$

where x_i represents a value of the random variable X and $P(x_i)$ represents the associated probability, and the products are summed for every possible value of X.

The next activity, Shooting Free Throws, asks students to make comparisons and distinguish between the expected value and the most likely outcome.

Shooting Free Throws

Goals

- Use simulation to investigate expected value in both a binomial situation and a nonbinomial situation
- Distinguish between the expected value and the most likely outcome

Materials and Equipment

- A copy of the activity pages for each student (or pair of students)
- Materials for simulations—cards, random number tables, graphing calculators with a random number function (or other software capable of generating random numbers, such as the Random Number Generator applet), or
- Binomial distribution simulation software, such as the Binomial Distribution Simulator applet (for the part of the activity that deals with two-shot fouls)

pp. 105–8

Discussion

In this activity, students work individually or in pairs with a scenario about Lisa, a high school basketball player who has recently been successful in 60 percent of her shots at the foul line. Assuming that Lisa's foul-shot percentage remains constant at 60 percent, students consider Lisa's likelihood of making 0, 1, or 2 successful shots in each of the two types of foul-shot situations in basketball—the one-and-one opportunity and the two-shot opportunity. The activity takes students step by step to a comparison of these different foul-shot situations with respect to the expected value per opportunity for Lisa.

Students are also asked to assume that the outcome of each shot is independent of the outcome of any other shot. As they discuss the problem, they may express concerns about the independence of free-throw outcomes. Whether or not the outcomes are independent is an open question; authors addressing the issue have argued both for and against independence. Emphasize to your students that they are working under the assumption that the probability of making each shot is independent of the results of previous shots. If students want to modify the probabilities to investigate what happens when the shots are not independent, they will quickly see that the situation becomes much more complicated!

The activity asks students to make predictions and then simulate trials of one-and-one and two-shot opportunities. Students focus first on the one-and-one situation. Simulating this situation draws students' attention to the fact that in a one-and-one opportunity the number of foul shots is not fixed in advance. Many students will be surprised to discover that making zero successful shots is the most likely outcome for a free-throw shooter like Lisa, with a success rate of 60 percent. Students correctly think of a 60 percent shooter as a player who

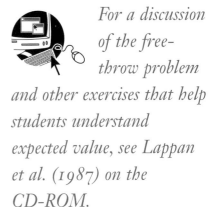

For a discussion of the free-throw problem and other exercises that help students understand expected value, see Lappan et al. (1987) on the CD-ROM.

This activity has been adapted from Lappan et al. (1987).

succeeds in making more than half of the free throws that she or he takes.

The sample space for the outcomes of a one-and-one foul-shot opportunity consists of a missed shot (0 successful shots), a successful shot followed by a missed shot (1 successful shot), and a successful shot followed by a successful shot (2 successful shots). If we use M to represent "missed shot" and S to represent "successful shot," we can denote the sample space as {M, SM, SS}. The tree diagram in figure 5.2 shows the probabilities of the outcomes in this sample space.

Fig. **5.2.**

Tree diagram of the probabilities of one-and-one outcomes for a player whose free-throw success rate is 60 percent

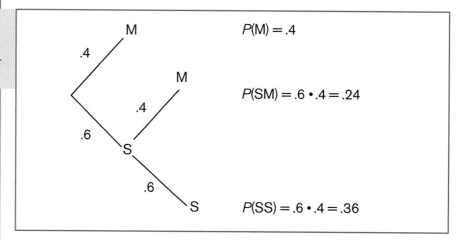

See Larkey, Smith, and Kadane (1989) on the CD-ROM for a discussion of independence versus "hot hands" in free-throw shooting. Gilovich, Vallone, and Tversky (1985) have also examined the topic.

The probability of making zero successful shots is simply the probability of missing the first shot, or $1 - .6$, or $.4$. Making one successful shot results from scoring on the first shot and missing the second one; the probability of this outcome is $.6 \cdot .4$, or $.24$. The probability of making two successful shots is $.6 \cdot .6$, or $.36$. Though it is true that making zero successful shots is less likely than making *at least* one successful shot, zero successful shots is more likely than either of the other two outcomes when they are considered individually.

Letting X be a random variable representing the number of points that Lisa obtains on a one-and-one opportunity, we can now calculate the expected value as follows:

$$E(X) = 0(.4) + 1(.24) + 2(.36) = 0 + .24 + .72 = .96$$

This value is likely to be lower than your students predict on the basis of intuition. Because Lisa's free-throw rate is 60 percent, students will probably expect that the points that Lisa scores in a one-and-one situation will average more than 1 over time.

In the second part of the activity, students focus on two-shot free-throw situations. Contrasting the one-and-one situation with the two-shot opportunity helps clarify for the students what is really going on. Students' predictions about the outcomes of two-shot free throws are usually more accurate than their predictions about one-and-one shots. For most students, thinking about the outcomes associated with a fixed number of events is easier than thinking about the outcomes associated with a variable number of events.

When two foul shots are awarded, the most likely number of successful shots is one. This result is based on the following probability distribution (see also the tree diagram in fig. 5.3):

If your students' predictions about the outcomes of two-shot free throws are more accurate than their predictions about one-and-one shots, ask them why they think this is so.

Number of successful shots	0	1	2
Probability	.16	.48	.36

Thus, for a 60 percent shooter, the expected value associated with two foul shots is 1.20:

$$E(X) = 0(.16) + 1(.48) + 2(.36) = 0 + .48 + .72 = 1.20$$

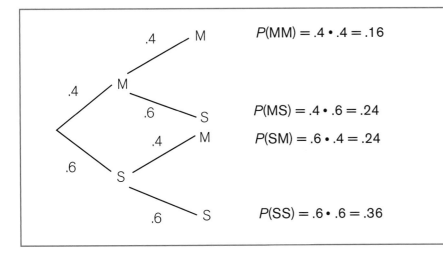

$P(MM) = .4 \cdot .4 = .16$

$P(MS) = .4 \cdot .6 = .24$

$P(SM) = .6 \cdot .4 = .24$

$P(SS) = .6 \cdot .6 = .36$

Fig. 5.3.

Tree diagram of the probabilities of two-shot outcomes for a player whose free-throw success rate is 60 percent

Class discussions about this activity can provide opportunities for teachers to review procedures and concepts related to probabilities of independent events. Also, this activity gives students an opportunity to see that the expected value does not have to be a possible value of the random variable. Having students explain how and why this makes sense can help them think more clearly about the concept of expected value as a long-term average outcome.

It is important for students to understand that the expected value does not have to be a possible value of the random variable.

Expected Values for Hitting Streaks in Baseball

The next activity, 39-Game Hitting Streak, applies the concept of expected value to hitting streaks in baseball—strings of consecutive games in which a player gets at least one hit in every game. The activity looks at the remarkable 39-game streak of Major Leaguer Paul Molitor in 1987 and probes the likelihood of such a streak for a hypothetical player hitting as well as Molitor was during that season.

39-Game Hitting Streak

Goal

Use the concept of expected value, as well as a simulation, to investigate a problem with a geometric distribution

Materials and Equipment

pp. 109–11

- A copy of the activity pages for each student (or pair of students)
- Materials for simulations—random number tables, graphing calculators with a random number function (or other software capable of generating random numbers, such as the Random Number Gererator applet), or
- Geometric probability simulation software, such as the Geometric Distribution Simulator applet

Discussion

The activity 39-Game Hitting Streak uses probability and expected value to evaluate how likely or unlikely Paul Molitor's 39-game hitting streak would be for a hypothetical batter of comparable ability. Students can work individually or in pairs to investigate the expected value, or average length over the long run, of a string of consecutive games with at least one hit per game for such a player. As they work, students may be surprised to discover that this problem belongs to the "wait-until" type.

Suppose that students let S be a random variable representing the length of a hitting streak—that is, the number of consecutive games with at least one hit in every game. At first glance, students might think that S is a random variable with a geometric distribution. On closer inspection, however, they will see that they are "waiting until" the player has a game without a hit. So the geometrically distributed random variable related to this situation, denoted by X, must represent the game number of the first game without a hit.

A streak of length 1 occurs when the player has a game with at least one hit followed by a game without a hit. So $X = 2$ when $S = 1$. The probability of a one-game streak is expressed as $P(S = 1)$ and is calculated as follows:

$$P(S = 1) = P(\text{at least 1 hit in game 1}) \cdot P(\text{no hit in game 2})$$
$$= (.784) \cdot (.216) \approx .169.$$

Note that $P(\text{no hit in 3 at-bats}) = P(\text{no hits in a game}) = (.6)^3 = .216$, and $P(\text{at least 1 hit in 3 at-bats}) = P(\text{at least 1 hit in a game}) = 1 - P(\text{no hits in 3 at-bats}) = 1 - (.6)^3 = .784$. A streak of length 2 occurs when the player has two games in a row with at least one hit followed by a game without a hit. The probability of this occurring is $P(S = 2) = (.784)^2 \cdot (.216) \approx .133$.

The probability that a player with a constant .400 batting average will have a 39-game hitting streak like the one for which Paul Molitor is famous is $P(S = 39) = (.784)^{39} \cdot (.216) \approx .000016$. This result suggests that Molitor's accomplishment was extremely unusual.

Students may be surprised to discover that evaluating the likelihood of Paul Molitor's streak is a "wait until" problem.

Students should note that even a 5-game streak has a very low probability (less than .07) for players of Molitor's caliber, yet streaks of such a length occur with sufficient frequency that they are not even considered newsworthy. As students discuss these very small probabilities, it is important that they continue to interpret them as long-term relative frequencies, providing information about what would be expected from many players of Molitor's talent over many seasons and many games.

Students should observe, in fact, that the probability of a streak of any specific length is small. This observation could provide a good opportunity to discuss the fact that if you are attempting to assess how unusual a particular outcome is, you might obtain useful additional information by looking at the probability of that outcome *or one that would be even more impressive*. For example, to assess how unusual is a streak of length 5, students might find it useful to look at the probability of a streak lasting at least five games. This probability can be calculated as follows:

$$P(S \geq 5) = 1 - P(S < 5)$$
$$= 1 - [P(S = 0) + P(S = 1) + P(S = 2) + P(S = 3) + P(S = 4)]$$
$$= 1 - [.216 + .784 \bullet .216 + (.784)^2 \bullet .216 + (.784)^3 \bullet .216$$
$$+ (.784)^4 \bullet .216]$$
$$\approx .30$$

Thus, a streak of five games or more is not so unlikely.

In the situation of the player hitting .400, knowledge about infinite geometric series is required to compute the expected value of a hitting streak analytically. (The expected value is approximately 3.63 for a .400 hitter who gets three at-bats per game.) All students can use simulations to estimate the mean length of hitting streaks that players like Molitor could be expected to have. Performing simulations will heighten students' awareness that even though probabilities associated with specific streaks may be low, longer streaks than students would expect do typically occur.

In the second part of the activity, students assume that the .400 hitter gets four at-bats in a game instead of just three. They recompute the probability of a 39-game hitting streak and perform a new simulation to estimate the expected value of a hitting streak in the new situation. Here the probability of the player getting at least one hit in a game is .8704, so the probability of a 39-game hitting streak increases, to approximately .00058, and the expected value for streak length also increases, to approximately 6.7.

Even the highest reasonable batting average and a high estimate of the constant number of hits per game give results that show Molitor's accomplishment as very, very special. As a concluding activity in class, have your students discuss and perhaps debate the assumptions of independence made throughout the activity.

Conclusion

This chapter gives only a brief introduction to expected value. Though this topic has customarily been reserved for courses focused on probability or statistics, all secondary students should know how to calculate and interpret expected value in simple cases, as *Principles and Standards* recommends. In discussing the activities in this chapter, as in discussing the other activities in the book, teachers should emphasize that the results of simulations and computations provide information about the long-run behavior of a random variable.

NAVIGATING *through* PROBABILITY

Looking Back and Looking Ahead

We use probability constantly in making everyday decisions, even though it defies intuition in many instances. Children encounter rudiments of probability at very early ages in questions like "Is it going to rain tomorrow?" Young students can consider simple outcomes, classifying them as *certain, likely, equally likely, unlikely,* or *impossible.* They can apply these first concepts of likelihood to games played with spinners or dice, and they can use them in deciding whether or not the games are fair. These explorations give students early indications that probability and data analysis are closely intertwined.

As children move through elementary school, they begin to quantify the likelihood of various events, launching the lengthy process of bringing mathematical precision to their ideas of uncertainty. Students' understanding of a close connection between data analysis and probability deepens as they gather data to test their predictions about outcomes. By tossing fair coins again and again and recording the results, for example, elementary school students often see that their preconceived ideas about the likelihood of coins landing heads up are at odds with the reality, as represented by their data.

Middle school students extend the process of quantifying probability, and they now begin to understand probability more abstractly, as the ratio of successful outcomes to the total number of outcomes. As they pursue their earlier work with spinners and dice, they discover meaningful connections between chance in the game settings and uncertainty in the real world. All the while, the data that they collect continue to challenge their intuitions about the likelihood of events.

As students enter high school, these intuitions about probability remain imprecise, but now they can be honed by explorations of probability through two systematic approaches. Both approaches extend ideas that students have encountered in their previous investigations of probability as a ratio, but the first approach builds more concretely and directly on students' earlier work with data. This approach interprets probabilities as long-run relative frequencies, computed from actual or simulated data gathered in many, many trials of probability experiments. The second approach, which is more abstract and formal, involves analyzing outcomes theoretically and calculating probabilities on the basis of the theoretical analysis.

This book has provided activities that allow students to use and compare these two approaches directly. The first approach calls on the students to use simulation and simulation technology as tools for gathering data and obtaining *experimental probabilities*. The second approach requires the students to draw on set theory and ideas related to combinatorics to obtain *theoretical probabilities*. The results from each approach reinforce and confirm the results from the other, thus consolidating and refining students' understanding of and intuitions about probability.

Moreover, as the students work through the activities, they encounter new, complex concepts, including *independence* and *expected value*, and they have opportunities to work directly with these ideas. They also discover classes of probability problems that result in a binomial or geometric distribution, and they investigate problems of these types.

In addition, and perhaps more important, the book has shown how to present these complex probability concepts in real-world settings. The activities let students use probability to model actual situations mathematically and discover such phenomena as independent events and conditional probability in natural, everyday contexts. Some of the situations presented are far too complex to be studied in all of their intricacies, but the simplified models that the book suggests allow students to gain an understanding of the associated probabilities and work meaningfully with them.

The book is intended to give you valuable resources to amplify and supplement the probability expectations set out in the Data Analysis and Probability Standard in *Principles and Standards for School Mathematics* (NCTM 2000). By offering your students experience with the ideas and techniques presented in these pages, you will prepare them to advance to careers in a variety of fields, including mathematics, psychology, sociology, economics, and business. Most important, you will give your students the skills that they will need to make sense of chance in numerous situations in their everyday adult lives, thus increasing their control over their destinies.

NAVIGATIONS SERIES

GRADES 9–12

NAVIGATING *through* PROBABILITY

Appendix

Blackline Masters and Solutions

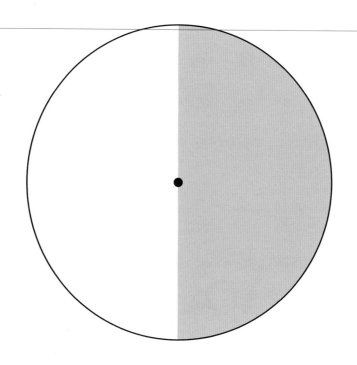

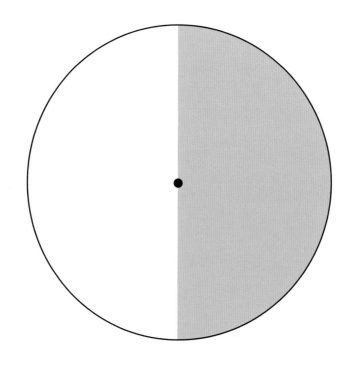

Is It Fair?

Name _____

Two fair spinners are part of a carnival game. A player wins a prize only when both arrows land in the shaded areas after each spinner has been spun once. James is playing the game.

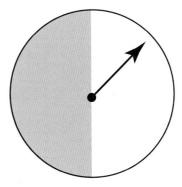 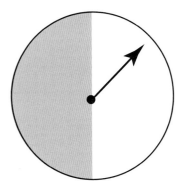

1. James thinks that he has a 50-50 chance of winning. Do you agree or disagree with James? _____ Why?

2. If you played the game 10 times, how many times would you expect to win? _____

3. Working with a partner, use actual spinners or simulation software to gather data on 10 games with spinners like those pictured. Record your results in any way that you wish.

4. *a.* If you played the game another 10 times, how many times would you expect to win? _____

   b. Is this prediction the same as your first prediction for 10 games in number 2? _____ Why, or why not?

5. *a.* On the next page, use the frequency graph labeled "10 Games" to display the data that you gathered in number 3. Then use technology (simulation software or calculator packages) to gather data on 20 games. Graph your results on the frequency graph labeled "20 Games." Repeat this process for 50 games and 100 games, completing the appropriate frequency graph in each case.

   b. What observations, if any, can you make about these graphs?

This activity is based on a problem that appeared in the 1996 National Assessment of Educational Progress and was subsequently released to the public.

Name _____

10 Games

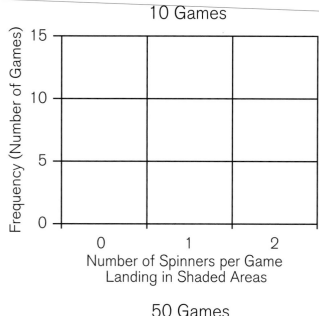

Number of Spinners per Game
Landing in Shaded Areas

20 Games

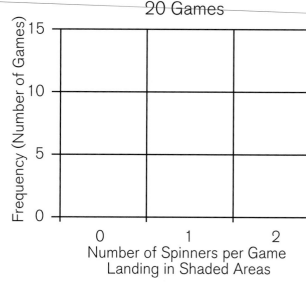

Number of Spinners per Game
Landing in Shaded Areas

50 Games

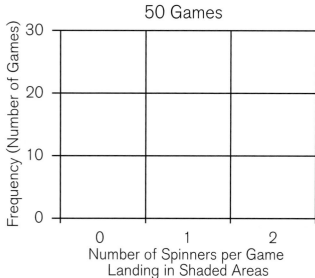

Number of Spinners per Game
Landing in Shaded Areas

100 Games

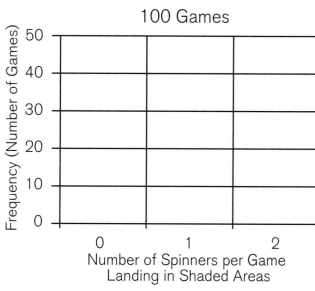

Number of Spinners per Game
Landing in Shaded Areas

6. *a.* Now that you have explored the spinner game a little more thoroughly, what do you think is the chance that both spinners will land in the shaded areas in this game? _____

   b. Explain why you think so.

   c. If you played the game 1000 times, about how many times would you expect both spinners to land in the shaded areas? _____

   d. Explain your thinking.

Spinning in Circles

Name _____

Consider the pictured spinner:

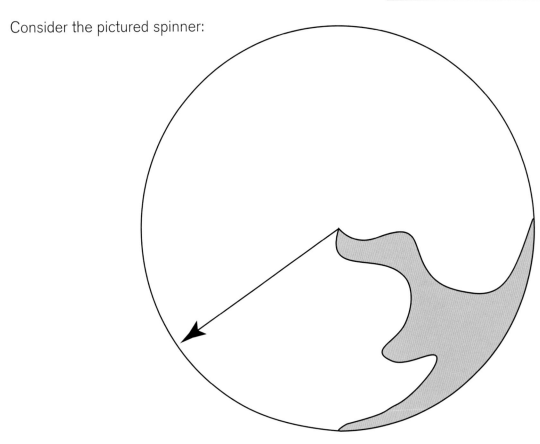

1. If you spun this spinner, do you think that the tip of the arrow would be likely to land in the shaded region? _____ Why, or why not?

2. A *probability* is a number between 0 and 1 that describes how likely it is that a particular outcome will occur. A probability of 0 represents an outcome that never occurs, and a probability of 1 represents an outcome that always occurs. If you spun the pictured spinner, which do you think would be closest to the probability that the tip of the arrow would land in the shaded area? _____

    a. 0   *b.* 1/10   *c.* 1/4   *d.* 1/2   *e.* 1

    Explain the reason for your selection.

3. Make a spinner arrow by bending the outside edge of a paper clip back so that it points in the opposite direction, as shown. (The length of your spinner arrow should be equal to the radius of the spinner disk, or 2 $\frac{1}{8}$ inches .)

    Use a pencil or pen to hold the looped end of the reshaped paper clip in place at the center of the pictured spinner disk. Try a few practice spins. Ignore the arrow that is drawn on the spinner and

Spinning in Circles (continued)

Name _____

instead use the end of the paper clip to determine the outcome of each spin. Now you are ready to investigate the probability that the tip of the spinner arrow will land in the shaded area.

4. The sample table, which shows the results of 3 spins, illustrates how you should complete table 1.

Sample table. *Cumulative Results of Spins*

Spin	In Shaded Area (Y = Yes, N = No)	Cumulative Number of Spins in Shaded Area	Cumulative Number of Spins	Proportion of Spins in Shaded Area
1	N	0	1	$0/1 = 0$
2	Y	1	2	$1/2 = .5$
3	N	1	3	$1/3 \approx .33$

Spin the spinner 20 times, and complete table 1 in the same way, by recording each outcome and updating your cumulative results, as shown. Remember to use the *tip of the paper clip* to determine whether the outcome of a spin is shaded or white, and note that each outcome appears as a yes (Y) or no (N) in the second column. After each spin, also update the numbers in the third and fifth columns of the table, referring to the sample as necessary.

Table 1

Cumulative Results of Spins

Spin	In Shaded Area (Y = Yes, N = No)	Cumulative Number of Spins in Shaded Area	Cumulative Number of Spins	Proportion of Spins in Shaded Area
1			1	
2			2	
3			3	
4			4	
5			5	
6			6	
7			7	
8			8	
9			9	
10			10	
11			11	
12			12	
13			13	
14			14	
15			15	
16			16	
17			17	
18			18	
19			19	
20			20	

Navigating through Probability in Grades 9–12

Spinning in Circles (continued)

Name _____

5. In 20 spins, what proportion of the time did the tip of the spinner land in the shaded area? _____
How close is this value to the value that you selected in number 2 as the probability of such a spin?

6. Using your data from table 1, plot the twenty pairs (*Cumulative number of spins, Proportion of spins in shaded area)* on plot 1. Connect the points in your plot to help see the pattern.

Plot 1. *The Proportion of Spins in the Shaded Area against the Cumulative Number of Spins*

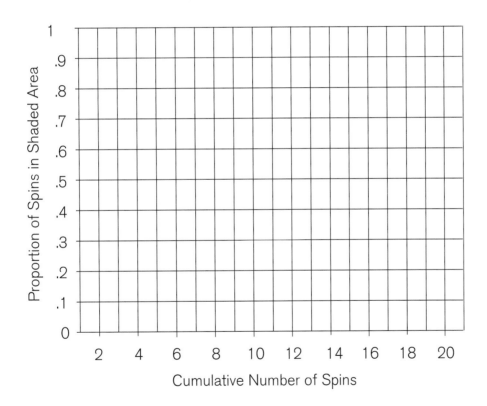

7. With guidance from your teacher, complete table 2 on the next page, which combines your results with the results of the other students in your class.

Spinning in Circles (continued)

Name _____

Table 2.

Cumulative Results of Spins (Class Data)

Student	Cumulative Number of Spins in Shaded Area	Cumulative Number of Spins	Proportion of Spins in Shaded Area
1		20	
2		40	
3		60	
4		80	
5		100	
6		120	
7		140	
8		160	
9		180	
10		200	
11		220	
12		240	
13		260	
14		280	
15		300	
16		320	
17		340	
18		360	
19		380	
20		400	
21		420	
22		440	
23		460	
24		480	
25		500	

8. Using the class data from table 2, construct plot 2 to display the pairs (*Cumulative number of spins, Proportion of spins in shaded area*). Connect the points in the plot to help see the pattern.

Spinning in Circles (continued)

Name _____

Plot 2. *The Proportion of Spins in the Shaded Area against the Cumulative Number of Spins (Class Data)*

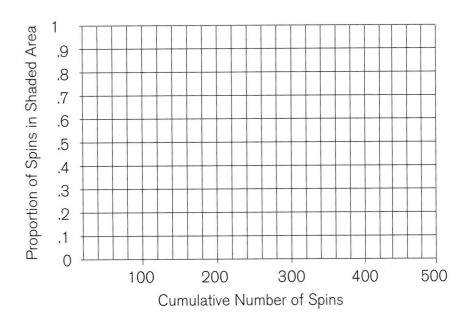

9. In Plot 1, the proportion of "shaded" outcomes is quite erratic over the course of only 20 spins. Plot 2 shows what happens over a longer run, with a much larger number of spins. The proportion of spins in the shaded area settles down, eventually becoming close to .25. Look again at the spinner and explain why the long-run proportion of spins in the shaded area is close to .25.

10. Probabilities can be interpreted as the long-run relative frequencies of outcomes. That is, a probability can be interpreted as the proportion of time that an outcome will occur in the long run, over many trials. Give a relative frequency-interpretation of the probability that this spinner will land in the shaded area.

11. For this spinner, the probability of a spin in the shaded area is .25.
    a. How does this value compare with the value that you selected in question 2?

    b. If you did not select 1/4 in question 2, describe the reasoning that led you to your original guess and, on the basis of what you have learned in this activity, explain why you have changed your mind.

A Matter of Taste

Names _____

_____

Jessica says that she can tell the difference between two name-brand colas, A and B. Her friend Luke is skeptical of this claim. To support her contention, Jessica asks Luke to give her a sample of one of the brands, chosen at random, in a plain paper cup. Jessica tastes it and correctly identifies the brand name. Luke gives Jessica another sample chosen at random, and *again* she correctly identifies the brand of cola.

- Would it be reasonable for Luke to suppose that Jessica really *could* distinguish between cola A and cola B both times, or could she have been just lucky?

- How many times might Jessica need to choose the correct brand twice in a row to convince Luke that she really can distinguish between the two brands?

Working with a partner, you will investigate these questions by estimating the probability that Jessica would be correct in each of two attempts if she really could not tell the two brands apart. In such a case, she really would be just guessing when she made her selections.

One member of your pair will act as Jessica and the other will act as Luke in a simulation of the scenario that assumes that Jessica was simply guessing. (You and your partner will switch roles later.)

Taking the roles of Luke and Jessica, you and your teammate will use two chips—one labeled "A" and the other labeled "B"—to represent cola A and cola B. Whoever is playing Luke should put the two chips in a small paper bag. Luke should shake the bag and then reach in and select one of the chips, without letting Jessica see which chip he has drawn. This process will represent Luke's random selection of cola A or cola B to put in a paper cup for Jessica to taste.

Whoever is playing Jessica should then guess which chip—i.e., cola A or cola B—Luke has selected. This guess will represent an attempt by Jessica to identify the cola without really being able to distinguish the taste of A from the taste of B.

After Jessica has guessed and Luke has shown the chip to reveal the guess as right or wrong, Luke should return the chip to the bag, shake it, and draw again for Jessica's second attempt at identifying the randomly selected cola. As before, Jessica should guess which chip (cola A or cola B) Luke has selected.

1. Record your outcomes in the first row of table 1. You and your partner have now completed one trial. Repeat the entire process nine more times to complete the first ten rows of the table. Then reverse roles and complete the next ten rows.

2. Consider the information from your twenty trials, as shown in table 1.

    a. In how many of these trials did Jessica guess correctly on both attempts? _____

    b. What proportion of the time did she guess correctly on both trials? _____

A Matter of Taste (continued)

Name _____

_____

Table 1

Results of 20 Simulated Taste Tests with Jessica Guessing

Trial	First Guess	First Chip	Second Guess	Second Chip	Both Correct? (Y = Yes, N = No)
1					
2					
3					
4					
5					
6					
7					
8					
9					
10					
11					
12					
13					
14					
15					
16					
17					
18					
19					
20					

3. Combine your data with the data generated by the other pairs of students in your class and compute the following:

   a. Number of pairs in the class: _____

   b. Total number of trials (20 × number of pairs): _____

   c. Total number of trials in which Jessica was successful on both attempts: _____

   d. Proportion of trials in which Jessica was successful on both attempts: _____

A Matter of Taste (continued)

Names $\underline{\hspace{8cm}}$

$\underline{\hspace{8cm}}$

4. The proportion calculated in 3(*d*) is the observed relative frequency of the outcome "both guesses correct." Since this proportion is based on a fairly large number of observations, it can be used as an estimate of the long-run relative frequency of this outcome, and therefore it can serve as an estimate of the outcome's probability. On the basis of your calculation in 3(*d*), what is the estimated probability that Jessica would guess correctly on both attempts?

5. Give a long-run relative-frequency interpretation of the estimated probability in number 4. On the basis of this estimated probability, write one or two sentences explaining whether Luke should be convinced that Jessica really can distinguish between cola A and cola B.

Discussion and Extension

1. Your work on the activity has probably shown you that it would not be all that unusual for a person who is just guessing to choose correctly on each of two attempts. Using an approach similar to the one you have just used, estimate the probability that someone who is guessing would be successful on each of three attempts.

2. What would it take to convince you that someone really could distinguish between cola A and cola B? That is, on how many attempts would Jessica need to be successful for Luke to be convinced that she really could distinguish between the two brands? Use a probability argument to justify your answer.

One-Boy Family Planning

Name _____

In 1979, when China instituted a policy limiting families to one child, some opponents of the policy proposed that it be revised to limit families to one boy rather than one child. Suppose that the Chinese government had accepted this idea and had instituted a one-boy policy allowing families to continue to have children until they had a boy. Would there be many large families in China as a result of this change to the policy? Would it be unusual to see a Chinese family with more than two children? With more than four children?

Use a six-sided die to generate simulated sibling groups that could result from a one-boy policy of family planning. Let a roll of the die represent a birth, with an even number indicating a girl (G) and an odd number indicating a boy (B). Thus, a roll giving GGB would simulate a sibling group of size 3, with the birth of a girl followed by the birth of another girl before the birth of a boy completed the group.

1. Why is this a reasonable way to simulate the birth of a baby of one gender or the other? (Be sure to mention probability in your explanation.)

2. Roll the die and observe whether the result represents the birth of a boy or the birth of a girl. If the roll simulates the birth of a boy, the resulting sibling group is complete. (Note that every complete group of children in a family is called a *sibling group,* even if it consists of only one child—a boy—with no siblings.) If your roll produces a girl, roll the die again, and observe whether the second roll results in the birth of a boy or the birth of a girl. Continue this process until the sibling group is complete (that is, a boy is obtained). Record the composition of your sibling group and the total number of children in the group in the first row of table 1. (For example, one possibility is GGGB, a sibling group of size 4.)

3. Now generate nineteen more sibling groups and record the information for each group in table 1.

4. Complete table 2 by combining your results with those obtained by the other members of your class to show the observed frequency of various sizes of sibling groups.

5. Sum the observed frequencies in table 2 to obtain the total number of sibling groups generated by the class. _____

This activity is based on Konold, Clifford, "Teaching Probability through Modeling Real Problems," *Mathematics Teacher* 87 (April 1994), pp. 232–35.

One-Boy Family Planning (continued)

Name _____

Table 1
Numbers of Children in 20 Simulated Sibling Groups under a One-Boy Policy of Family Planning

Sibling Group	Group Composition	Total Number of Children
1		
2		
3		
4		
5		
6		
7		
8		
9		
10		
11		
12		
13		
14		
15		
16		
17		
18		
19		
20		

Table 2.
Observed Frequencies of Different-Sized Simulated Sibling Groups under a One-Boy Policy of Family Planning (Class Data)

Number of Children in Sibling Group	Observed Frequency	
1		
2		
3		
4		
5		
6		
7		
8		
9		

Name _____

6. Compute the observed relative frequency of each sibling group size by calculating

$$\frac{Number\ of\ sibling\ groups\ observed\ for\ the\ group\ size}{Total\ number\ of\ sibling\ groups}$$

Include the observed relative frequencies in table 2 by creating a third column under a new heading, "Observed Relative Frequency."

7. Use the observed relative frequencies that table 2 now shows to estimate the following probabilities:
   a. The probability that a couple following a one-boy family planning policy will have more than two children. _____
   b. The probability that a couple following a one-boy family planning policy will have more than four children. _____
   c. The probability that a couple following a one-boy family planning policy will have just one child.

   _____

8. Does the observed number of small sibling groups surprise you? _____
   Explain.

Spinner Templates for "Check Out *These* Spinners"

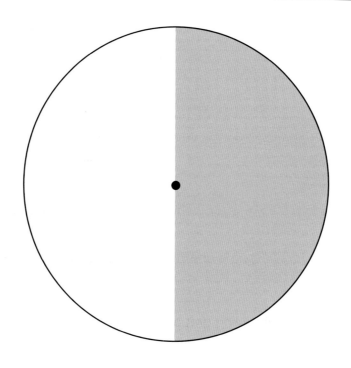

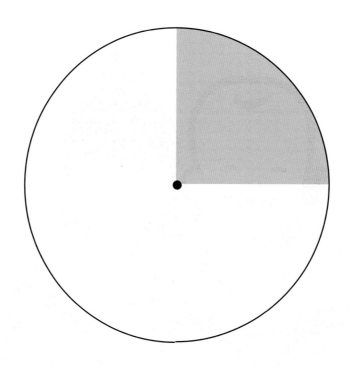

Navigating through Probability in Grades 9–12

Check Out *These* Spinners

Name _____

Consider the pictured spinners:

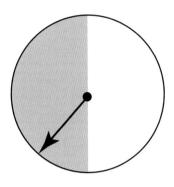 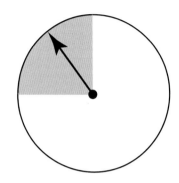

Suppose that you win a game if you spin each of these spinners one time and both arrows land in shaded areas.

1. What do you think your chance of winning this game would be? _____ Why?

2. If you played this game 50 times, about how many times would you expect to win? _____ Why?

3. Working with a partner, use spinners like those pictured and gather data on 50 games. What percentage of the time did both spinners land in shaded areas? _____

4. Gather data from enough other pairs of students to give you results from hundreds of games with the spinners. What percentage of the time did both spinners land in shaded areas? _____ How does this percentage compare with your prediction in number 1?

5. *a.* If you played the game 2000 times, how many times would you expect the first (one-half shaded) spinner to land in the shaded area? _____ Why?

   b. About how many of those spins in the shaded area would you expect to be paired with another spin in the shaded area on the second (one-quarter shaded) spinner? _____ Why?

Check Out *These* Spinners (continued)

Name _____

6. The number that you wrote in 5(*b*) of number 5 is the total number of games out of 2000 in which you would expect both spinners to land in shaded areas. What percentage of the 2000 games is that number? _____ What is the probability that both spinners will land in shaded areas? _____

7. What is the probability that the first spinner will land in the shaded area? _____ What is the probability that the second spinner will land in the shaded area? _____ How are these individual probabilities related to the probability that you gave in number 6 that *both* spinners will land in shaded areas?

Sounding an Alarm

Name _____

North High School hired the Safety-First Company to install smoke detectors in the school cafeteria. The company recommended installing three smoke detectors and claimed that if smoke appeared anywhere in the cafeteria, each of the smoke detectors would have a 75 percent chance of sounding an alarm.

1. What is your best guess of the probability that at least one of these detectors would sound an alarm if smoke appeared in the cafeteria? _____ Why do you think so?

A group of North High School students worked on the problem and listed the outcomes for the smoke detectors as follows: {0S, 1S, 2S, 3S}. This *sample space* indicates the numbers of smoke detectors that could sound if smoke appeared in the cafeteria. The students then assigned the following probabilities to the outcomes: $P(0S) = 1/4$, $P(1S) = 1/4$, $P(2S) = 1/4$, $P(3S) = 1/4$. The students concluded that if smoke appeared anywhere in the cafeteria, the probability that at least one smoke detector would sound would be 3/4, since they had assigned 1/4 as the chance that no smoke detector would sound.

2. *a.* What do you think of the North High School students' approach, and why?

   b. Would you list the outcomes in the sample space in the same way that the North High School students did? _____ If not, how would you list them?

   c. What probabilities would you assign for each of the following outcomes: 0S?_____ 1S? _____
   2S? _____ 3S? _____

   Explain.

3. *a.* Use the multiplication and addition principles to calculate the probability that at least one smoke detector would sound if smoke appeared in the cafeteria.

Sounding an Alarm (continued)

Name _____

b. How does your answer compare with your guess in number 1?

c. How does your answer compare with the decision of the group of North High School students, as presented in number 2?

Three-Dice Sums

Name _____

Suppose that you tossed three regular six-sided dice, and after each toss you found the sum of the numbers on the three dice.

1. *a.* List the possible sums for tossing three dice.

   b. What sum (or sums) would you expect as the most likely outcome(s)? _____
      As the least likely? _____

   c. Why would you think so?

2. Work with a partner and toss three dice 50 times.

   a. Record the sum of each toss.

(1) _____	(11) _____	(21) _____	(31) _____	(41) _____
(2) _____	(12) _____	(22) _____	(32) _____	(42) _____
(3) _____	(13) _____	(23) _____	(33) _____	(43) _____
(4) _____	(14) _____	(24) _____	(34) _____	(44) _____
(5) _____	(15) _____	(25) _____	(35) _____	(45) _____
(6) _____	(16) _____	(26) _____	(36) _____	(46) _____
(7) _____	(17) _____	(27) _____	(37) _____	(47) _____
(8) _____	(18) _____	(28) _____	(38) _____	(48) _____
(9) _____	(19) _____	(29) _____	(39) _____	(49) _____
(10) _____	(20) _____	(30) _____	(40) _____	(50) _____

   b. Use regular grid paper or a copy of "Graph the Frequencies of Three-Dice Sums" to make a graph that represents the number of times that each sum occurs (its frequency).

3. Compare your results with those of several other pairs of students. Pool your data with theirs so that you have the results of hundreds of trials of tossing three dice and summing the numbers. As a group, make a graph of the combined results on a second grid.

4. Compare your group's results with those of other groups.

Three-Dice Sums (continued)

Name _____

   a. On the basis of your data, what would you give as the probability of each of the possible sums?

   b. What would you identify as the most likely sum? _____

5. Probabilities of the three-dice sums can be determined by analyzing outcomes as well as by obtaining relative frequencies. Consider the following:

   a. What are the different ways in which three dice can give you a sum of 4?

   b. What is the probability that you will get a sum of 4? _____ Explain your thinking.

   c. What are the different ways in which three dice can give you a sum of 8?

   d. What is the probability that you will get a sum of 8? _____ Explain your thinking.

   e. What sum or sums are most likely to occur when you toss three dice?

   f. What is the probability that this sum or these sums occur?

6. Compare your work in question 5, where you analyzed outcomes, to your earlier work in questions 1–4 with relative frequencies. What observations can you make?

Graph the Frequencies of Three-Dice Sums

Name _____

Abby's Kennels

Name _____

Abby's Kennels recently offered an obedience-training course that enrolled 50 dogs. Thirty dogs were classified as "large," and 20 dogs were classified as "small," on the basis of their weights. At the end of the course, which consisted of five sessions, the owners of 15 dogs received certificates indicating that their dogs had passed the course.

1. From the information in the scenario, guess the number of dogs in each of the following categories:

    a. Number of large dogs that passed the course. _____

    b. Number of small dogs that passed the course. _____

2. Use your guesses to complete table 1.

Table 1
Conjectures about Obedience Course Results for Large and Small Dogs at Abby's Kennels

	Passed the Course	Did Not Pass the Course	Total
Large dogs			30
Small dogs			20
Total	15	35	50

You have been given three "mystery bags," labeled "X," "Y," and "Z," which simulate possible combinations of dogs and course results at Abby's Kennels. Each bag holds 50 chips. Thirty red chips represent the large dogs, and 20 blue chips represent the small dogs. In addition, 15 chips with stars (or another special marker) in each bag represent the dogs that passed the obedience course at Abby's Kennels.

3. Select one chip from bag X. In row 1 of table 2, check (✓) the descriptors of the dog that the chip represents. Repeat the procedure for chips from bags Y and Z, recording your results in tables 3 and 4. Return each chip to the appropriate bag, mix the chips, and repeat the process of selecting chips and recording descriptors until you have drawn at least 10 chips from each bag.

Abby's Kennels (continued)   Name _____

Table 2.
Descriptors of Dogs Represented by Chips Selected from Bag X

Selection Number	Large Dog (Red Chip)	Small Dog (Blue Chip)	Dog That Passed the Obedience Course (Chip with Star)
1			
2			
3			
4			
5			
6			
7			
8			
9			
10			

Table 3.
Descriptors of Dogs Represented by Chips Selected from Bag Y

Selection Number	Large Dog (Red Chip)	Small Dog (Blue Chip)	Dog That Passed the Obedience Course (Chip with Star)
1			
2			
3			
4			
5			
6			
7			
8			
9			
10			

Table 4.
Descriptors of Dogs Represented by Chips Selected from Bag Z

Selection Number	Large Dog (Red Chip)	Small Dog (Blue Chip)	Dog That Passed the Obedience Course (Chip with Star)
1			
2			
3			
4			
5			
6			
7			
8			
9			
10			

Abby's Kennels (continued)

Name _____

4. When you selected a chip representing a large dog, did you always put a check mark in one other category as well in the chart for—

    a. bag X? _____   *b.* bag Y? _____   *c.* bag Z? _____

5. When you selected a chip representing a dog that passed the obedience course, did you always put a check mark in one other category as well in the chart for—

    a. bag X? _____   *b.* bag Y? _____   *c.* bag Z? _____

6. Pool the results of your selections from each bag with the results of at least two other students who have been collecting data from other sets of mystery bags. Show the data cumulatively in table 5.

Table 5
Characteristics of Dogs Represented by Chips Selected from Bags X, Y, and Z

Dogs Selected from Bag X

Total Number of Selected Dogs	Large Dogs	Dogs That Passed the Course	Dogs That Were Large *and* Passed the Course
10 dogs			
20 dogs			
30 dogs			

Dogs Selected from Bag Y

Total Number of Selected Dogs	Large Dogs	Dogs That Passed the Course	Dogs That Were Large *and* Passed the Course
10 dogs			
20 dogs			
30 dogs			

Dogs Selected from Bag Z

Total Number of Selected Dogs	Large Dogs	Dogs That Passed the Course	Dogs That Were Large *and* Passed the Course
10 dogs			
20 dogs			
30 dogs			

Abby's Kennels (continued)

Name _____

Venn diagrams could be used to organize these data on large dogs and their results in the obedience course (passed or did not pass the course). The Venn diagrams labeled (*a*), (*b*), and (*c*) show three possible representations of the data, with circle L representing the set of large dogs and circle P representing the set of dogs that passed the course.

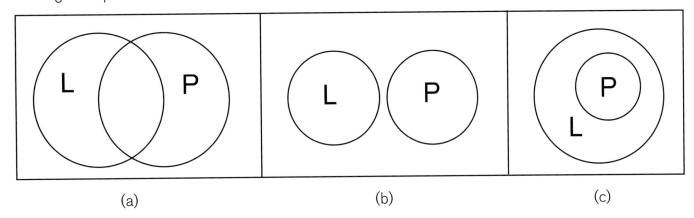

(a)   (b)   (c)

7. Reexamine the results that you tallied in table 5. Could any of the three Venn diagrams represent—

    a. Bag X? _____ Why, or why not?

    b. Bag Y? _____ Why, or why not?

    c. Bag Z? _____ Why or why not?

8. If 9 large dogs passed the course at Abby's Kennels, which Venn diagram(s) could not represent the total dog population at the kennel?_____ Why?

9. If 9 large dogs passed the course—

    a. how many small dogs passed the course? _____
    b. how many large dogs did not pass the course? _____
    c. how many small dogs did not pass the course? _____

Abby's Kennels (continued)

Name _____

10. Use the numbers from question 9 to complete table 6:

Table 6.

Obedience Course Results for Large and Small Dogs at Abby's Kennels

	Passed the Course	Did Not Pass the Course	Total
Large dogs			30
Small dogs			20
Total	15	35	50

Refer to the completed table to answer questions 11–16.

11. Interpreting probabilities as relative frequencies, what is the probability that a randomly selected dog would be—

   a. a large dog? _____

   b. a small dog? _____

   c. a dog that passed the course? _____

   d. a large dog that passed the course? _____

Two events A and B are considered *independent* if the probability of both A and B occurring in a single selection from a population is the product of the probability of the first event *times* the probability of the second event. This is represented symbolically as $P(A \cap B) = P(A) \cdot P(B)$.

12. Suppose that event A is "selecting a dog that passed the course" and event B is "selecting a dog that is large." What is the probability that both events A and B will occur in the selection of a single dog from the population of dogs summarized in table 6? Are the two events independent? Justify your answer by using the formula $P(A \cap B) = P(A) \cdot P(B)$.

13. Consider the 30 large dogs summarized in table 6. If you chose one dog from this population, what would be the probability that you would select a dog that had passed the course? _____

This probability is a *conditional probability*. It gives the likelihood of selecting a dog that passed the obedience course *given that* the selected dog is large. This probability is represented symbolically as $P(A|B)$, again with A standing for the event "selecting a dog that passed the course" and B standing for the event "selecting a dog that is large."

Abby's Kennels (continued)

Name _____

14. Consider only the 20 small dogs summarized in table 6 in question 10.

    a. What is the probability that one of these dogs passed the course? _____

    b. Is this probability a conditional probability? _____ Explain.

15. Table 6 organizes the 50 dogs by size and results from the obedience course. How do your conditional probabilities from questions 13 and 14 demonstrate that the event "selecting a dog with particular course results" ("passed the course" or "did not pass the course") is independent of the event "selecting a dog of a particular size" ("large" or "small")?

16. Suppose that a dog owner asked a trainer at Abby's Kennels if different obedience course results could be expected for large and small dogs. How do you think that this trainer should respond if the events were independent?

17. How would you expect the trainer to respond about different results for different sized dogs if Bag X represented the dogs at Abby's Kennels?

    If bag Z represented the dogs?

18. Return to table 1 (in question 2). Did your initial guesses indicate that the size and course results of a dog were independent? _____ Explain your answer.

Independent or Not Independent?

Name _____

Research studies suggest that the incidence of asthma is increasing at a rapid rate, especially among teenagers. Researchers do not agree on the exact causes of this condition or how to address its symptoms. Most medical studies, however, indicate that asthma is closely linked to environment, and research suggests that the most successful way to alleviate the suffering caused by asthma is to improve air quality. One of the worst air pollutants in the home environment is cigarette smoke. Research indicates that smoke-filled air triggers severe symptoms in asthma sufferers.

Students at South High School conducted a research study to investigate questions about asthma. They decided that data gathered through a school survey would help them explore a number of questions:

- Is air that is dirty from cigarette smoke more likely to be found in the home of an asthmatic student than in the home of a nonasthmatic student?
- What is the probability that an asthmatic student lives in a household with one or more smokers?
- Is this probability higher for an asthmatic student than it is for a nonasthmatic student?

Independent or not independent? That is the question! Responses from the 937 students attending South High School gave the following data:

- Number of students with asthma: 182
- Number of students living in households with one or more smokers: 395

The students used a two-way table like table 1 to organize their data.

Table 1

Household Composition (with or without Smokers) of Asthmatic and Nonasthmatic Students at South High School

	Households with One or More Smokers	Households without Smokers	Total
Asthmatic students	Cell 1	Cell 4	Cell 7
Nonasthmatic students	Cell 2	Cell 5	Cell 8
Total	Cell 3	Cell 6	Cell 9

1. What cells in this two-way table can you fill in with the numbers tallied from the survey forms? _____ Place the values in the correct cells of the table.

Independent or Not Independent? (continued)

Name _____

2. On the basis of the tallied information, which of the following probabilities can you calculate, and which can you not determine?

   a. The probability that a student selected at random from the students at this high school has asthma? _____

   b. The probability that a student selected at random from the students at this high school lives in a household with one or more smokers? _____

   c. The probability that a student selected at random from the students at this high school has asthma and lives in a household with one or more smokers? _____

   Go back and calculate each probability that you can determine, and if you cannot determine a probability, explain why.

3. Further examination of the survey results revealed that 113 South High School students had asthma *and* lived in households with one or more smokers.

   a. Use this information to complete table 1.
   b. Reconsider (*a*)–(*c*) in question 2. Are there any probabilities that you could not determine before that you can calculate now? _____ Compute the value of any such probabilities.

If the probability of an asthmatic student living in a household with one or more smokers is equal to the probability of a nonasthmatic student living in a household with one or more smokers, then being asthmatic and living in a household with one or more smokers are independent events. If the probabilities are not the same, then the events are not independent.

4. Seeing the two-way table "pulled apart" into separate rows may help clarify the situation. Consider the portion of the table shown:

	Households with One or More Smokers	Households without Smokers	Total
	Cell 1	Cell 4	Cell 7
Asthmatic students	113	69	182

Independent or Not Independent? (continued)

Name _____

Using these data from the row for "Asthmatic students," determine—

a. the probability that a randomly selected student with asthma lives in a household with one or more smokers. _____

b. the probability that a randomly selected student with asthma does not live in a household with one or more smokers. _____

5. In the same way, consider the row for "Nonasthmatic students" isolated from the row for "Asthmatic students":

	Households with One or More Smokers	Households without Smokers	Totals
	Cell 2	Cell 5	Cell 8
Nonasthmatic students	282	473	755

Using these data, determine—

a. the probability that a randomly selected nonasthmatic student lives in a household with one or more smokers. _____

b. the probability that a randomly selected nonasthmatic student lives in a household without smokers? _____

Questions 4 and 5 separated the information collected in the survey on the basis of the asthma status (asthmatic or nonasthmatic) of the students who completed the survey forms. The computed probabilities were based on the total number of students belonging to each row.

Consider selecting a South High School student at random and define the events A, $\overline{A}$, S, and $\overline{S}$ in the following way:

"A" is the event "selecting a student with asthma."

"$\overline{A}$" is the event "selecting a student without asthma."

"S" is the event "selecting a student who lives in a household with one or more smokers."

"$\overline{S}$" is the event "selecting a student who lives in a household without smokers."

6. The probabilities that you derived in questions 4 and 5 depend on whether a student has asthma or does not have asthma. They are *conditional* probabilities. Tell what each of the following conditional probabilities represents:

a. $P(S|A)$ _____

b. $P(S|\overline{A})$ _____

Independent or Not Independent? (continued)

Name _____

7. From the values summarized in the two-way table, determine the values of the following:

  a. $P(S|A) =$ _____

  b. $P(S|\overline{A}) =$ _____

8. From the data in table 1, determine $P(S)$, the probability that a randomly selected student from the total school population lives in a household with one or more smokers. _____

9. What does it mean if $P(S|A) \neq P(S)$? (Explain in the context of the South High School students' survey on asthma status and living in a household with or without smokers.)

10. Use the data in table 1 to answer the following questions:

  a. What is the value of $P(A \cap S)$?

  b. If A and S are independent events, then $P(A \cap S) = P(A) \cdot P(S)$.
     Are the two events A and S independent? _____ Why, or why not?

Discussion and Extension

1. When the South High School students began their research, they thought that students with asthma would be more likely than students without asthma to live in households with one or more smokers. Do the data from the surveys support this hypothesis? (Use the probabilities that you calculated in the activity to explain your answer.)

2. A major goal of the South High School students' project was to determine if it might be possible to alleviate the symptoms of asthmatic students by altering the air quality in their home environments. What do you think the students at South High School could do as a result of their research?

What's the Probability of a Hit?

Name _____

Suppose that a baseball player has a constant batting average of .400. Thus, in any turn at bat, the player has a constant probability of getting a hit, or *P*(H), of .4, and a constant probability of *not* getting a hit, or *P*(N), of .6.

1. Consider the digits 0–9. Let any of the digits 0–3 represent a hit (H) and any of the digits 4–9 represent "no hit" (N).

    a. How does such an assignment of digits represent the player's batting average of .400?

    b. Use a random number table or a graphing calculator with a random number function (or other appropriate software) to obtain three random digits to stand for the results of three at-bats for this player. Record your random digits. _____

    c. Using "H" for "hit" and "N" for "no hit," show the sequence of results for your three simulated at-bats. _____

2. Imagine that you had 20 such simulated sets of three at-bats for this player. In how many of those 20 sets would you expect the player to have gotten at least 2 hits? _____ Why?

3. *a.* Using "H" and "N" again to stand for "hit" and "no hit," respectively, construct the sample space (the set of all possible outcomes) for three times at bat. _____

    b. Which outcome or outcomes include at least 2 hits? _____

    c. Compare your sample space with the sample spaces constructed by some of your classmates. Do you all agree on the sample space for the problem? _____

4. *a.* Compute the probabilities of each of the individual outcomes in your sample space. (*Hint:* The multiplication principle may be helpful.)

What's the Probability of a Hit? (continued)

Name _____

b. Use these probabilities to calculate the theoretical probability that a baseball player would get at least 2 hits in three times at bat if the player's probability of getting a hit remained constant at $P(H) = .4$.

Repeating the process that you followed in question 1, gather data on 20 sets of three at-bats for the player with a constant .400 batting average.

5. a. Record the number of hits in each set of three at-bats.

(1) _____	(5) _____	(9) _____	(13) _____	(17) _____
(2) _____	(6) _____	(10) _____	(14) _____	(18) _____
(3) _____	(7) _____	(11) _____	(15) _____	(19) _____
(4) _____	(8) _____	(12) _____	(16) _____	(20) _____

b. On the basis of your simulated data for 20 at-bats, what is the probability that the player will get at least 2 hits in three times at bat? _____

c. How does this result, which is a relative frequency based on simulated data, compare with your guess in question 2?

d. How does your result from 5(b) compare with your calculation in question 4?

6. Compare the results of your simulations of 20 sets of three at-bats with those of several of your classmates. How close is the probability that you derived for 2 hits in three at-bats to the probabilities that they derived from their data?

Again use the process that you followed in question 1, this time gathering data from 50 simulated sets of three times at bat for the player with a constant batting average of .400.

What's the Probability of a Hit? (continued)

Name _____

7. a. Record the number of hits in each set of three at-bats.

(1) _____	(11) _____	(21) _____	(31) _____	(41) _____
(2) _____	(12) _____	(22) _____	(32) _____	(42) _____
(3) _____	(13) _____	(23) _____	(33) _____	(43) _____
(4) _____	(14) _____	(24) _____	(34) _____	(44) _____
(5) _____	(15) _____	(25) _____	(35) _____	(45) _____
(6) _____	(16) _____	(26) _____	(36) _____	(46) _____
(7) _____	(17) _____	(27) _____	(37) _____	(47) _____
(8) _____	(18) _____	(28) _____	(38) _____	(48) _____
(9) _____	(19) _____	(29) _____	(39) _____	(49) _____
(10) _____	(20) _____	(30) _____	(40) _____	(50) _____

b. In your 50 sets of three at-bats, how many times did the player get zero hits? _____
One hit? _____ Two hits? _____ Three hits? _____

c. Using the grid shown, construct a graph of the frequency of the number of hits (0, 1, 2, or 3) that occurred in your 50 sets of three at-bats.

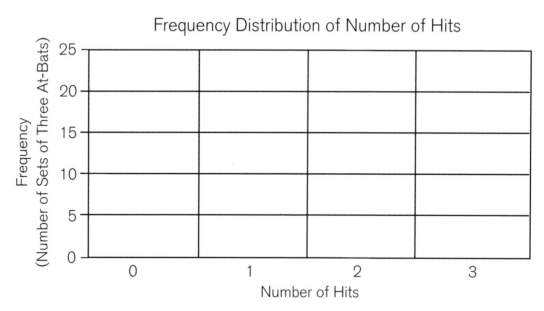

Frequency Distribution of Number of Hits

d. On the basis of your data for 50 sets, what is the probability that the player gets at least 2 hits in three at-bats? _____

e. How does your result in 7(d) compare with your guess in question 2?

Name _____

f. How does your result in 7(d) compare with your calculation in question 4?

g. How does your result in 7(d) compare with the result from your simulation of 20 sets of three at-bats in question 5?

8. Compare the results of your simulations of 50 sets of three at-bats with those of several of your classmates. How close is the probability that your derived this time for 2 hits in three at-bats to the probabilities that they derived from their data?

How Likely Is That Jury?

Name _____

A woman is coming to trial in a controversial case involving domestic violence, and jury selection is about to begin. Assume that in the pool of prospective jurors the ratio of men (M) to women (W) is one to one and remains constant throughout the jury selection process. Thus, $P(M)$ and $P(W)$ remain constant at .5 for each juror selected from the pool, and each selection is independent of every other one. Prospective jurors are selected until a 12-member jury panel is complete.

1. *a.* How many total outcomes are there in the sample space for the associated binomial probability distribution of 12 jurors who are men or women? _____

   b. List those outcomes that have 11 or more men.

2. Pick one of the outcomes with 11 men. Use the multiplication principle to compute the probability of that outcome.

3. *a.* Let *X* be the random variable "the number of men on a jury." Compute the probability that at least 11 men would be called initially to a jury. That is, find $P(X \geq 11)$. (*Hint:* The addition principle can help with this problem).

   b. On the basis of your analysis, how likely would the woman who is coming to trial be to obtain a jury with 11 or more men on it by chance? _____

   c. If you were an attorney for a defendant in a case in which 11 or 12 men were initially called to the jury, would you raise a question? _____ Why, or why not?

How Likely Is That Jury? (continued)

Name _____

Use a random number table or a graphing calculator with a random number function (or other appropriate software) to simulate a sample of 40 juries, each with 12 people. (You could use the digits 0–4 for W, and 5–9 for M).

4. *a.* Record the number of men in each of your 40 simulated juries.

(1) _____	(9) _____	(17) _____	(25) _____	(33) _____
(2) _____	(10) _____	(18) _____	(26) _____	(34) _____
(3) _____	(11) _____	(19) _____	(27) _____	(35) _____
(4) _____	(12) _____	(20) _____	(28) _____	(36) _____
(5) _____	(13) _____	(21) _____	(29) _____	(37) _____
(6) _____	(14) _____	(22) _____	(30) _____	(38) _____
(7) _____	(15) _____	(23) _____	(31) _____	(39) _____
(8) _____	(16) _____	(24) _____	(32) _____	(40) _____

b. On the basis of your data, what is the probability of obtaining a jury with at least 11 men on it?

_____

c. How does your result in 4(*b*) compare with the probability for a jury of at least 11 men that you calculated in question 2?

Consecutive Hits–
Consecutively Hitless

Name _____

Suppose that a baseball player has a constant batting average of .400. Thus, in any turn at bat, the player has a constant probability of getting a hit, or $P(H)$, of .4 and a constant probability of not getting a hit, or $P(N)$, of .6.

1. Without calculating, make an intuitive guess for each of the following:

   a. The probability that the player's first hit is on the fourth at-bat. _____

   b. The probability that the player's first turn at bat without a hit is the fourth at-bat. _____

Working with a partner or in a group, use a random number table or a graphing calculator with a random number function (or other appropriate software) to collect simulated data for a player who continues to come to bat *until* obtaining the first hit. For instance, you could let any of the digits 0–3 stand for a hit (H) and any of the digits 4–9 stand for "no hit," or "not a hit" (N). Thus, for example, the digits 7842 would stand for "no hit, no hit, no hit, hit," or the sequence NNNH, with the first hit occurring on the fourth at-bat.

2. Repeat the process of generating a sequence "until the first hit" to create 50 such simulated sequences.

   a. For each of your sequences, record the number of simulated at-bats until the first hit.

(1) _____	(11) _____	(21) _____	(31) _____	(41) _____
(2) _____	(12) _____	(22) _____	(32) _____	(42) _____
(3) _____	(13) _____	(23) _____	(33) _____	(43) _____
(4) _____	(14) _____	(24) _____	(34) _____	(44) _____
(5) _____	(15) _____	(25) _____	(35) _____	(45) _____
(6) _____	(16) _____	(26) _____	(36) _____	(46) _____
(7) _____	(17) _____	(27) _____	(37) _____	(47) _____
(8) _____	(18) _____	(28) _____	(38) _____	(48) _____
(9) _____	(19) _____	(29) _____	(39) _____	(49) _____
(10) _____	(20) _____	(30) _____	(40) _____	(50) _____

   b. On the basis of your data, what is the probability that a batter with a constant .400 average would have to wait until the fourth at-bat to get the first hit?

   c. How does your result from 2(b) compare with your guess in 1(a)?

Consecutive Hits–Consecutively Hitless (continued)

Name _____

3. *a.* Again generate 50 sequences of numbers, this time recording the number of simulated at-bats until the first turn in which the player *fails* to get a hit.

(1) _____   (11) _____   (21) _____   (31) _____   (41) _____
(2) _____   (12) _____   (22) _____   (32) _____   (42) _____
(3) _____   (13) _____   (23) _____   (33) _____   (43) _____
(4) _____   (14) _____   (24) _____   (34) _____   (44) _____
(5) _____   (15) _____   (25) _____   (35) _____   (45) _____
(6) _____   (16) _____   (26) _____   (36) _____   (46) _____
(7) _____   (17) _____   (27) _____   (37) _____   (47) _____
(8) _____   (18) _____   (28) _____   (38) _____   (48) _____
(9) _____   (19) _____   (29) _____   (39) _____   (49) _____
(10) _____   (20) _____   (30) _____   (40) _____   (50) _____

b. On the basis of your data, what is the probability that a batter with a constant .400 average would not fail to get a hit in any at-bat until the fourth one?

c. How does your result from 3(*b*) compare with your guess in 1(*b*)?

Now consider the sample space for four at-bats by the player.

4. *a.* Let *X* be the random variable *Number of turns at bat until the player gets the first hit.* Use the multiplication principle to find $P(X = 4)$.

b. Let *Y* be the random variable *Number of turns at bats until player fails to get a hit.* Use the multiplication principle to find $P(Y = 4)$.

c. How do your probability calculations in 4(*a*) and (*b*) compare to the probabilities obtained from your simulations in parts 2(*b*) and 3(*b*)?

One-Girl Family Planning

Name(s)_____

Suppose that an overpopulated country decides to mandate family planning. The country is matriarchal, and girls have a higher status than boys. After heated debate of a proposed one-child policy, the country adopts a more popular one-girl policy. This policy allows couples to have children until they have a girl, but then they must have no more children.

Assume that all couples capable of having children will continue to do so until they produce a girl. On average, how many children would you expect families to have in this country?

1. Predict the average number of children that families would have under the one-girl policy? _____ Explain why you have chosen this number.

2. Consider the simulated data in table 1, compiled by students in another class. (Note that a complete group of children in a family is called a *sibling group,* even if it consists of only one child with no siblings.)

Table 1

Observed Frequencies of Different-Sized Simulated Sibling Groups under a One-Girl Policy of Family Planning (Data Gathered in Another Class)

Number of Children in a Sibling Group	Observed Frequency
1	242
2	128
3	59
4	32
5	24
6	8
7	3
8	2
9	2

What is the mean number of children in these simulated sibling groups?

You could also use your own data to calculate the mean number of children in sibling groups under a one-girl policy of family planning, by conducting a simulation with cards, dice, a random-number table, a graphing calculator with a random number function, or other appropriate software. If you simulate data of your own, record them in table 2, and use them to calculate the mean number of children in sibling groups under a one-girl policy of family planning. (Note that this table appears under a slightly different title as table 2 in the activity One-Boy Family Planning. If you completed that activity, you could use your data from that table here, since the probabilities of male and female births are both close enough to .5 to be treated as equal.)

One-Girl Family Planning (continued)

Name(s) _____

Table 2

Observed Frequencies of Different-Sized Simulated Sibling Groups under a One-Girl Policy of Family Planning (Data Gathered in Our Class)

Number of Children in a Sibling Group	Observed Frequency
1	
2	
3	
4	
5	
6	
7	
8	
9	

3. Under the one-girl policy, *Number of children in a family* is a random variable with a geometric distribution and a probability of success—the birth of a girl—equal to 1/2. Thus, you can calculate theoretical probabilities associated with sibling groups of all possible sizes. Complete table 3 to display a portion of the probability distribution for this random variable.

Table 3

Theoretical Probabilities of Sibling Groups of Different Sizes

Number of Children in a Sibling Group	Probability
1	
2	
3	
4	
5	
6	
7	
8	
9	
10	

One-Girl Family Planning (continued)

Name(s) _____

4. *a.* Use the information from your partial probability distribution in question 3 to calculate the expected mean number of children in a very large number of sibling groups (500, 1000, or 10 000, for example).

b. Compare your result with the mean number of children in the simulated sibling groups.

5. Look back at the computations you performed with theoretical probabilities in question 4. Can you express your work in the form $1 \cdot P(1) + 2 \cdot P(2) + 3 \cdot P(3) + \ldots$? _____

This expression can be used to determine the mean number of children that would be expected in many sibling groups, or the *expected value,* directly from a probability distribution. In general, the expected value of a random variable X is computed by multiplying each possible value of the random variable by its associated probability and summing all products.

Symbolically, the expected value of X is denoted as $E(X)$ and defined as $E(X) = \Sigma\, x_i P(x_i)$, where x_i represents a value of the random variable X, $P(x_i)$ represents the associated probability, and the products are summed for every possible value of X.

Shooting Free Throws

Name(s) _____

Lisa is a starting player on her high school basketball team. She typically gets fouled several times in a game. Some fouls result in one-and-one opportunities, and others result in two-shot chances. In a one-and-one situation, Lisa attempts a free-throw shot. If she succeeds in making the shot, she earns the chance to attempt a second shot. However, if Lisa misses the first shot of a one-and-one opportunity, she does not get a second attempt. By contrast, in a two-shot foul opportunity, Lisa gets a second free throw no matter what happens on her first shot. In recent games, Lisa has been successful in 60 percent of her free throws. Assume that Lisa's probability of making a successful free-throw shot remains constant at .6 and that the outcome of each shot is independent of the outcome of every other shot.

1. Without doing any calculations, predict the most likely number of foul shots (zero, one, or two) that Lisa succeeds in making when she goes to the line for a one-and-one opportunity. _____

2. Design a simulation in which each trial models a one-and-one foul-shot opportunity for Lisa. Describe your simulation.

3. Use your simulation to conduct 40 trials, each representing a different one-and-one opportunity for Lisa. Record the number of simulated successful free throws in each trial.

Trial	Number of Successful Free Throws	Trial	Number of Successful Free Throws	Trial	Number of Successful Free Throws
1		15		29	
2		16		30	
3		17		31	
4		18		32	
5		19		33	
6		20		34	
7		21		35	
8		22		36	
9		23		37	
10		24		38	
11		25		39	
12		26		40	
13		27			
14		28			

This activity has been adapted from Lappan, Glenda, Elizabeth Phillips, William M. Fitzgerald, and M. J. Winter, "Area Models and Expected Value," *Mathematics Teacher* 80 (November 1987): 650–54.

Shooting Free Throws (continued)

Name(s) _____

a. On the basis of your 40 trials, what is the most likely outcome for Lisa in a one-and-one opportunity? _____

b. How does this outcome compare with your prediction in question 1?

c. Using the results of your 40 trials, calculate Lisa's mean number of successful free throws per one-and-one opportunity.

4. a. What theoretical probabilities are associated with Lisa's making zero, one, and two successful shots when she goes to the line for a one-and-one foul-shot opportunity? Calculate these theoretical probabilities.

b. Each successful foul shot earns Lisa's team 1 point. Use the definition of expected value to calculate Lisa's mean number of points per opportunity for one-and-one foul situations.

c. How does your calculation in 4(b) compare with your result from your simulation in 3(c)?

Now consider Lisa's free-throw results in two-shot free-throw opportunities.

5. a. Without doing any calculations, predict the most likely number of shots (zero, one, or two) that Lisa succeeds in making when she goes to the line for a two-shot opportunity. _____

b. Without doing any calculations, predict the mean number of successful free throws Lisa makes per two-shot free-throw opportunity over the course of a season. _____

Shooting Free Throws (continued)

Name(s) _____

6. Design a simulation in which each trial models a two-shot free-throw opportunity for Lisa. Describe your simulation.

7. Use your simulation to conduct 40 trials, each representing a different two-shot opportunity for Lisa. Record the number of simulated successful free throws in each trial.

Trial	Number of Successful Free Throws	Trial	Number of Successful Free Throws	Trial	Number of Successful Free Throws
1		15		29	
2		16		30	
3		17		31	
4		18		32	
5		19		33	
6		20		34	
7		21		35	
8		22		36	
9		23		37	
10		24		38	
11		25		39	
12		26		40	
13		27			
14		28			

a. On the basis of your 40 trials, what is the most likely outcome for Lisa in a two-shot free-throw opportunity? _____

b. How does this outcome compare with your prediction in 5(a)?

c. Using the results of your 40 trials, calculate Lisa's mean number of successful free throws per two-shot opportunity.

d. How does this result compare with your prediction in 5(b)?

Shooting Free Throws (continued)

Name _____

a. What theoretical probabilities are associated with Lisa's making zero, one, and two shots when she goes to the line for a two-shot free-throw opportunity? Calculate these theoretical probabilities.

b. As before, each successful foul shot earns Lisa's team one point. Use the definition of expected value to calculate Lisa's mean number of points per opportunity for two-shot foul situations.

c. How does your calculation in 8(*b*) compare with your result from your simulation in 7(*b*)?

9. Compare one-and-one and two-shot free-throw opportunities with respect to the expected value per opportunity for the points that Lisa will score in the two situations.

39-Game Hitting Streak

Name(s) _____

In 1987, Major League baseball player Paul Molitor batted nearly .400 and succeeded in stringing together 39 consecutive games in which he got at least one hit. Suppose that a player's batting average remains constant at .400 throughout a season, and assume that the outcome of each at-bat is independent of the outcome of every other at-bat. How unusual would a hitting streak such as Molitor's be?

1. Suppose that the player gets three at-bats in a game. The probability that the player will get no hits in a game is .216, and the probability that he or she will get at least 1 hit is .784.

   a. Verify these probabilities.

   b. Calculate the probability of a one-game, a two-game, and a three-game hitting streak for the player.

   c. Calculate the probability of a streak as long as Molitor's for this player. That is, calculate the player's probability of putting together 39 consecutive games with at least one hit in every game, followed by a hitless game that breaks the streak.

   d. Compare this probability to the player's probability of a three-game streak.

Probabilities associated with specific outcomes give only part of the information that is helpful in determining long-term behavior. The expected value, or the average length of a hitting streak for a player like Molitor over the long run, can provide additional information to indicate how special Molitor's streak really was. Since you are interested in a random variable that has infinitely many values, the formula for expected value is complicated to apply. However, a simulation can give you data that you can use to estimate the expected value.

2. Design a simulation in which each trial models a hitting streak—that is, a string of consecutive games in which the player gets at least one hit, followed by a hitless game.

   a. Describe your simulation.

39-Game Hitting Streak (continued)

Name(s) _____

b. Conduct 40 trials of your simulation, being careful to record the length of each hitting streak (that is, the number of consecutive games in which the player gets a hit) rather than the number of the first game without a hit.

Trial	Length of Hitting Streak	Trial	Length of Hitting Streak	Trial	Length of Hitting Streak
1		15		29	
2		16		30	
3		17		31	
4		18		32	
5		19		33	
6		20		34	
7		21		35	
8		22		36	
9		23		37	
10		24		38	
11		25		39	
12		26		40	
13		27			
14		28			

3. a. Using the results of your simulation, calculate the mean length of a hitting streak for the player.

b. Compare your mean with that of other students in your class and with Molitor's 39-game streak. From the simulation results in your class, how unusual or surprising do you think Molitor's streak really was?

39-Game Hitting Streak (continued)

Name(s) _____

4. Suppose we assume that the player with the constant batting average of .400 gets four at-bats in a game instead of just three. Recalculate the probability of a 39-game hitting streak for the player.

5. Design a simulation in which each trial models a hitting streak for the player with four at-bats in a game. Conduct 40 trials, and use the results as before, to estimate the expected value for the length of a hitting streak for the player.

Trial	Length of Hitting Streak	Trial	Length of Hitting Streak	Trial	Length of Hitting Streak
1		15		29	
2		16		30	
3		17		31	
4		18		32	
5		19		33	
6		20		34	
7		21		35	
8		22		36	
9		23		37	
10		24		38	
11		25		39	
12		26		40	
13		27			
14		28			

Mean length of a hitting streak = _____

6. Throughout this activity, you have assumed that the outcome of each at-bat is independent of the outcomes of every other at-bat and that getting a hit in one game is independent of getting a hit in another game. Do you have confidence that these assumptions are valid? _____ Why, or why not?

Solutions to Blackline Masters

Solutions for "Is It Fair?"

1. The game does not offer players a 50-50 chance that both spinners will land in the shaded areas. However, many students will believe that it does until they investigate more carefully.

2. Students' answers will vary at this exploratory stage. Students who think that the game is fair are likely to expect that they would win about 4 to 6 times in 10 games. Other students might suggest that they would expect 2 or 3 wins, especially if they suspect that the likelihood of a win is 25 percent.

3. Asking students to share the ways in which they recorded the outcomes from the spins can elicit some interesting information. Students may create different types of lists or graphs. These different approaches sometimes shed light on the problem for other students.

4. *a* and *b*. You can use these questions to give students an opportunity to discuss their predictions with the whole class and explain their reasoning. Data gathered on only 10 games (in question 3) will show a great variety of results. Some students may believe that the game is fair on the basis of "confirming evidence" of 4 or 5 wins in 10 games with the spinners. Thus, in (*b*), they might respond that they have not changed their predictions. Other students will change their predictions on the basis of the data obtained in question 3. These differences can lead to a discussion and a call for more data (see question 5).

5. *a*. Sample results for 10, 20, 50, and 100 games are given in figure 0.1*a–d* in the text. Results will vary, but again it is interesting for students to compare them across groups, or pairs, or individually (however you have organized the process of data gathering in your class).

   b. You can use this question as another opportunity for students to discuss and share their ideas. Students will make a variety of observations about their graphs, possibly noting that the frequency of both spinners landing in the shaded areas is not half of the time or even close to it. They might observe that as the number of games increases, the frequency of having both spinners land in the shaded areas seems to be settling down to around 1/4.

6. *a–d*. Students may suggest that about 250 of the 1000 games would result in both spinners landing in shaded areas. They might say that they would expect this outcome to occur about a quarter of the time. There might still be some argument or discussion about whether the game is fair, depending on the results of the students' experiments. However, by now the evidence should be quite strong that the game is not fair. It is also possible that some students will base their reasoning on a list of all possible outcomes, such as SS, SW, WS, WW, with W representing a spin landing on white and S representing a spin landing in the shaded area. If students did not think of these four different possibilities at the beginning of the activity, they may have become aware of them while they were actually spinning. Often students will "see" the four different outcomes as they spin the spinners.

Solutions for "Spinning in Circles"

Note: Actual responses from students will vary depending on the outcomes of their spins.

1. Most students will think it is unlikely that the tip of the arrow will land in the shaded region.

2. Many students will choose a fraction like 1/10 because the area of the shaded region is about 1/10 of the area of the circle. Some will correctly pick 1/4 by focusing on the circle perimeter.

4. Table 1 will look something like the following:

Spin	In Shaded Area (Y = Yes, N = No)	Cumulative Number of Spins in Shaded Area	Cumulative Number of Spins	Proportion of Spins in Shaded Area
1	N	0	1	.00
2	N	0	2	.00
3	N	0	3	.00
4	N	0	4	.00
5	Y	1	5	.20
6	Y	2	6	.33
7	N	2	7	.29
8	Y	3	8	.38
9	N	3	9	.33
10	N	3	10	.30
11	Y	4	11	.36
12	Y	5	12	.42
13	N	5	13	.38
14	N	5	14	.36
15	N	5	15	.33
16	N	5	16	.31
17	N	5	17	.29
18	Y	6	18	.33
19	N	6	19	.32
20	N	6	20	.30

5. For the sample data shown in the preceding solution, the proportion of the time that the tip of the spinner landed in the shaded area is .30. Students who chose a fraction like 1/10 as the estimated probability of the time that the spinner would land in the shaded area in question 2 may be surprised that the proportion is so high.

6. Plot 1 here shows the sample data from the table in the solution to question 4:

Plot 1. The Proportion of Spins in the Shaded Area against the Cumulative Number of Spins

7 and 8. With class data, table 2 and plot 2 might look something like the following:

Student	Cumulative Number of Spins in Shaded Area	Cumulative Number of Spins	Proportion of Spins in Shaded Area
1	6	20	.300
2	12	40	.300
3	15	60	.250
4	21	80	.263
5	26	100	.260
6	29	120	.242
7	34	140	.243
8	38	160	.238
9	45	180	.250
10	49	200	.245
11	51	220	.232
12	55	240	.229
13	60	260	.231
14	63	280	.225
15	69	300	.230
16	73	320	.228
17	76	340	.224
18	82	360	.228
19	88	380	.232
20	95	400	.238
21	100	420	.238
22	104	440	.236
23	109	460	.237
24	118	480	.246
25	123	500	.246

Plot 2. The Proportion of Spins in the Shaded Area against the Cumulative Number of Spins (Class Data)

9. The long-run proportion of "shaded" outcomes is about 1/4 because the tip of the spinner arrow lands on the perimeter of the circle, and about 1/4 of the perimeter of the circle is shaded.

10. If this spinner is spun many, many times, the tip of the spinner arrow will land in the shaded region about 1/4 of the time.

11. *a* and *b*. If students selected the correct probability in question 2, the results of their spins should confirm their choice. If students selected a fraction like 1/10 on the basis of an estimate of the area of the shaded region, the results should help them see that it is only the tip of the spinner arrow, and thus the perimeter of the circle, that matters.

Solutions for "A Matter of Taste"

Note: Students' responses will vary depending on the outcomes of their simulations.

1. Table 1 should look something like the following:

Trial	First Guess	First Chip	Second Guess	Second Chip	Both Correct? (Y = Yes, N = No)
1	A	B	A	A	N
2	B	A	B	B	N
3	A	A	A	B	N
4	B	B	A	A	Y
5	A	B	A	A	N
6	B	A	A	A	N
7	B	B	B	B	Y
8	A	B	B	B	N
9	B	B	B	A	N
10	A	A	B	A	N
11	B	B	B	B	Y
12	B	B	A	A	Y
13	A	A	B	B	Y
14	B	A	B	A	N
15	B	A	B	A	N
16	B	A	A	B	N
17	B	B	B	B	Y
18	A	A	B	B	Y
19	B	B	B	A	N
20	A	B	B	B	N

2. *a.* For the sample data in table 1, Jessica was correct on both attempts 7 times.

   b. The proportion of the time she guessed correctly on both trials was 7/20 = .35.

3. With a class of 26 students, the class data might look something like the following:

   a. Number of pairs in the class: 13

   b. Total number of trials (20 × number of pairs): 260

   c. Total number of trials in which Jessica was successful on both attempts: 72

   d. Proportion of trials in which Jessica was successful on both attempts: .277

   Note: The true probability of guessing correctly on two trials is .25. The proportion obtained from the class data is an estimate of this probability.

4. On the basis of the sample class data shown, the estimated probability is .277.

5. On the basis of the estimated probability here (.277), if Jessica could not really distinguish between the two colas, she would still be likely to be correct on both of two successive trials about 27.7 percent of the time, just by chance. Since Jessica would be correct on both trials by chance this often, even when she was just guessing, the fact that she happened to be right in two trials of cola should not convince Luke that she really can distinguish between cola A and cola B.

Discussion and Extension

1. The probability of correctly guessing the correct brand on three successive trials is .125. Class estimates based on a simulation of a three-trial experiment should result in estimates that are close to this value.

2. Most students will conclude that it would take more than three correct identifications to convince them that someone could really distinguish between the two brands of cola. In the long run, three correct guesses in a row still happen about 12 percent of the time just by chance.

Solutions for "One-Boy Family Planning"

Note: Students' responses will vary depending on the outcomes of their simulations.

1. This method of representing a birth results in equal probabilities of a girl (.5) and a boy (.5).

2 and 3. Table 1 might look like the following:

Sibling Group	Group Composition	Total Number of Children
1	GGB	3
2	GB	2
3	GB	2
4	B	1
5	B	1
6	GGB	3
7	GGB	3
8	B	1
9	B	1
10	GB	2
11	B	1
12	B	1
13	GGGGB	5
14	GGGB	4
15	GB	2
16	GGB	3
17	GB	2
18	B	1
19	B	1
20	GB	2

4. For a class of 25 students, table 2 might look like the following:

Number of Children in Sibling Group	Observed Frequency	Observed Relative Frequency
1	242	.484
2	128	.256
3	59	.118
4	32	.064
5	24	.048
6	8	.016
7	3	.006
8	2	.004
9	2	.004

5. For the sample class data in table 2, the total number of sibling groups is 500.

6. See the third column, Observed Relative Frequency, which has been added to table 2 above.

7. For the sample class data in table 2—

   a. $1 - (.484 + .256) = 1 - .74 = .26$

   b. $.048 + .016 + .006 + .004 + .004 = .078$

   c. $.484$

8. Most students will be surprised by the fact that about 7/8 of the families have three children or fewer.

Solutions for "Check Out *These* Spinners"

1. As discussed in the text, some students might think the chance of winning is 3/8; some might believe it is 3/4; some might know that it must be less than the chance of winning in the spinner game presented in the introductory activity, Is It Fair? There the probability of landing in the shaded region was 1/2 for each spinner. Your class might also include students who multiply 1/2 by 1/4 to get the correct result.

2. Students' answers will vary. In general, students will use their probability guesses to estimate the number of wins in 50 games.

3. Answers will vary. It would be interesting to list all the winning percentages from all the pairs of students in the class and to look at the range of those percentages.

4. It would also be interesting to look at the range of winning percentages from the various groups after pairs of students have pooled their data. This process would provide opportunities to discuss the variation that occurs in results when a probability experiment is repeated and to look at what happens to the range of winning percentages as the numbers of trials increase.

5. a. About 1000, since you would expect the first spinner to land in the shaded region about half the time.

   b. About 250, since 250 is 1/4 of the 1000 spins that you would expect in the shaded region on first spinner.

6. 12.5 percent, or 1/8 of the games.

7. The probability that the first spinner will land in the shaded area is 1/2; the probability that the second spinner will land in the shaded area is 1/4. Using the multiplication principle for independent events, the probability that both spinners will land in shaded areas is 1/2 • 1/4, or 1/8.

Solutions for "Sounding an Alarm"

1. Students' answers will vary.

2. *a.* Some students might think the North High School students' approach is fine; others might say that the probability has to be higher than 3/4 because it is possible that two or more smoke detectors would sound.

    b. The sample space could be listed as sequences of three smoke detectors, with each one either sounding (S) or not sounding (N): {SSS, SSN, SNS, NSS, NNS, NSN, SNN, NNN}.

    c. Both the multiplication principle and the addition principle are helpful in finding these probabilities. By the multiplication principle, $P(0S) = P(NNN) = (.25) \cdot (.25) \cdot (.25) \approx .016$. By the addition principle, $P(1S) = P(SNN) + P(NSN) + P(NNS) = 3 \cdot [(.75) \cdot (.25) \cdot (.25)] \approx .140$. Similarly, $P(2S) = 3 \cdot [(.75) \cdot (.75) \cdot (.25)] \approx .422$, and $P(3S) = (.75)^3 \approx .422$.

3. *a.* The only outcome without at least one smoke detector sounding is NNN.
    $P(NNN) = .016$, so P(at least one detector sounding) $= 1 - .016 = .984$.

    b. The probability is a lot higher than most students will have estimated. (There are clear benefits to having multiple smoke detectors.)

    c. The probability is also significantly higher than the group of students at North High School estimated.

Solutions for "Three-Dice Sums"

1. *a.* Lists will include all the whole numbers from 3 to 18.

    b and *c.* Students' answers will vary. Some students might expect 7 to be the most likely sum, since it is the most likely outcome for the sum of two dice. Other students might pick numbers "in the middle" between 3 and 18, recalling what occurs for two dice. Some students might not be familiar with the results of the two-dice problem, so the sums of two dice could be a good follow-up investigation for them.

2. Students' graphs will vary, but certain trends should be common to all of them, since the most likely sums are in the middle, and sums at both ends of the graph are quite unlikely to occur.

3 and 4. It can be interesting to compare different students' graphs to look at the variation that occurs in the results when a probability experiment is repeated by different people.

5. *a.* If we think of a toss of three dice as giving a sequence of outcomes, there are three different ways in which we can obtain a sum of 4 in a toss of three dice: (2,1,1), (1,2,1), and (1,1,2). (Having dice in three different colors might help explain this reasoning.)

    b. There are $6 \cdot 6 \cdot 6$, or 216, different sequences that are possible for tossing three dice. If the dice are fair, you would expect each of those sequences to have the same chance of occurring, or 1/216. Thus, $P(4) = 3/216 \approx .014$.

    c. A sum of 8 could be obtained as follows: (6,1,1), (1,6,1), (1,1,6), (2,1,5), (2,5,1), (5,2,1), (5,1,2), (1,5,2), (1,2,5), (4,3,1), (4,1,3), (3,1,4), (3,4,1), (1,3,4), (1,4,3), (4,2,2), (2,4,2), (2,2,4), (3,3,2), (3,3,2), and (2,3,3).

    d. There are 21 different combinations of the three dice that will have a sum of 8; thus $P(8) = 21/216 \approx .097$.

    e. The sums 10 and 11 are the most likely to occur when three dice are tossed.

    f. $P(10) = P(11) = 27/216$.

6. In comparing the frequency distributions that they have made, students will probably encounter a good deal of variability. In all likelihood, they will also find a good deal of variation when they compare the theoretical probabilities with their experimental probabilities. They may see this variability "settling down" as the sample sizes increase in their probability experiments.

Solutions for "Abby's Kennels"

1. Students' answers will vary. This question is intended to be a discussion question. Students may express an opinion that you can use as an early indication of their understanding of situations in which events are independent or not independent.

2. Students' answers will vary. Verify that the table agrees with the guesses that the students recorded in question 1.

3. Students' data will vary. The 10 selections from each bag should be made by each student or by small groups of 2 or 3 students. Students will use the results to conjecture about the composition of the bags and thus of the dog population.

4. The answer is no for all three bags. In the case of 4(a) or 4(c), students could possibly obtain an unusual sample, in which all the large dogs selected would be dogs that passed the obedience course (for Bag X) or all the small dogs selected would be dogs that passed the obedience course (for Bag Z). As a result, it is important to analyze students' answers according to the selections that the students recorded in question 3.

5. *a.* Yes. The descriptor "large dog" would also be checked.
   b. No.
   c. Yes. The descriptor "small dog" would also be checked.

6. Students' answers will vary according to their combined results. Analyze answers according to the selections that the students recorded.

7. *a.* Yes. Venn diagram (c) indicates that each dog that passed the obedience course was a large dog. It could also indicate that not all large dogs passed the course.
   b. Yes. Venn diagram (a) indicates that both large dogs and small dogs could have passed the obedience course.
   c. Yes. Venn diagram (b) indicates that no dog that passed the obedience course was large. It could also indicate that not all small dogs were dogs that passed the obedience course.

8. If 9 large dogs passed the obedience course, then 6 small dogs also passed the obedience course. Therefore, Venn diagram **(b)**, which shows that no large dogs passed the obedience course, and diagram **(c)**, which shows that only large dogs passed the course, could not be used to represent this situation.

9. *a.* 6 small dogs passed the course.
   b. 21 large dogs did not pass the course.
   c. 14 small dogs did not pass the course.

10. Table 6

Obedience Course Results for Large and Small Dogs at Abby's Kennels

	Passed the Course	Did Not Pass the Course	Total
Large dogs	9	21	30
Small dogs	6	14	20
Total	15	35	50

11. *a.* 30/50 = .6, or 60 percent
    b. 20/50 = .4, or 40 percent
    c. 15/50 = .3, or 30 percent
    d. 9/50 = .18, or 18 percent

12. $P(A) = .3$, or the probability of selecting a dog that passed the obedience course.
    $P(B) = .6$, or the probability of selecting a large dog.
    $P(A \text{ and } B)$, on the basis of the two-way table, is 9/50 or .18
    $P(A \text{ and } B)$, on the assumption of independence, is
    $$P(A \cap B) = P(A) \cdot P(B) = (.3) \cdot (.6) = .18$$

13. 9/30 = .3, or 30 percent

14. *a.* 6/20 = .3, or 30 percent
    b. Yes. The probability is derived from the population of small dogs (the condition of size was stated).

15. The conditional probabilities are equal, indicating that in both cases the event that was given as a condition (selecting a dog of a particular size) had no effect on the occurrence of the second event (selecting a dog that passed the obedience course). Thus, the equality of the conditional probabilities suggests that the events are independent.

16. The trainer should probably indicate that an obedience course could be expected to have the same results for large or small dogs.

17. If Bag X represented the dog population, then the trainer should indicate that large dogs achieve the best results from an obedience course. If Bag Z represented the dog population, then the trainer should indicate that small dogs achieve the best results from an obedience course.

18. Students' answers will vary according to the students' responses to question 2. If a student's guesses indicated conditional probabilities that were equal for selecting a dog that passed the obedience course from the population of large dogs and for selecting a dog that passed the obedience course from the population of small dogs, then the student hypothesized that the events were independent. Otherwise, the student supposed that the events were not independent.

Solutions for "Independent or Not Independent?"

1. With the data that the students have been given at this point in the problem, they can fill in cells 3, 6, 7, 8, and 9 of the table:

Table 1

Household Composition (with or without Smokers) of Asthmatic and Nonasthmatic Students at South High School

	Households with One or More Smokers	Households without Smokers	Total
Asthmatic students	Cell 1	Cell 4	Cell 7 182
Nonasthmatic students	Cell 2	Cell 5	Cell 8 755
Total	Cell 3 395	Cell 6 542	Cell 9 937

Cells 1, 2, 4, and 5 represent counts of the responses to the survey questions regarding smoking *and* asthma. At least one of cells 1, 2, 4, and 5 must be known to complete the table.

2. *a.* Yes; $\frac{182}{937} \approx .194$, or 19.4 percent.

   b. Yes; $\frac{395}{937} \approx .422$, or 42.2 percent.

   c. No; this probability cannot be derived from the given data.

3. Given that 113 students have asthma and live in households with one or more smokers, students can now complete the table:

Table 1

Household Composition (with or without Smokers) of Asthmatic and Nonasthmatic Students at South High School

	Households with One or More Smokers	Households without Smokers	Total
Asthmatic students	*Cell 1* 113	*Cell 4* 69	*Cell 7* 182
Nonasthmatic students	*Cell 2* 282	*Cell 5* 473	*Cell 8* 755
Total	*Cell 3* 395	*Cell 6* 542	*Cell 9* 937

All of the probabilities in question 2 can now be determined. The probability for 2(*c*) is

$$\frac{113}{937} \approx .125, \text{ or } 12.5 \text{ percent.}$$

4. *a.* $\frac{113}{182} \approx .621$, or 62.1 percent.

   b. $\frac{69}{182} \approx .379$, or 37.9 percent. This probability can also be explained as the complement of the probability in 4(*a*).

5. *a.* $\frac{282}{755} \approx .374$, or 37.4 percent.

   b. $\frac{473}{755} \approx .626$, or 62.6 percent. This probability is the complement of the probability in 5(*a*).

6. *a.* The probability of selecting a student who lives in a household with one or more smokers, given that the student has asthma.
   b. The probability of selecting a student who lives in a household with one or more smokers, given that the student does not have asthma.

7. *a.* $\frac{113}{182} \approx .621$, or 62.1 percent.

   b. $\frac{282}{755} \approx .374$, or 37.4 percent.

8. $\dfrac{395}{937} \approx .422$, or 42.2 percent.

9. The probability of selecting a student who lives in a household with one or more smokers from the students who have asthma is higher than the probability of selecting a student who lives in a household with one or more smokers from the total population of the school. Understanding this question indicates that students are beginning to understand when two events are not independent.

10. *a.* On the basis of the data in the table, $P(A \cap S) = \dfrac{113}{937} \approx .125$, or 12.5 percent.

b. The two events are not independent, as demonstrated by the following substitutions:

$$P(A \cap S) = P(A) \bullet P(S) = \left(\dfrac{182}{937}\right)\left(\dfrac{395}{937}\right)$$

This expression is approximately equal to (.194) • (.422), or .082, or 8.2 percent. These results indicate that the two events are not independent. For the data represented in the table, selecting a student who lives in a household with one or more smokers is more likely to occur when the selection is made from the group of asthmatic students than when it is made from the group of all students at South High School.

Discussion and Extension

1. The survey data do support the hypothesis of the South High School students. The events are not independent. The data indicate that living in a household with one or more smokers is more likely for asthmatic students at this high school than it is for students from the whole student population at the school.

2. Students' answers will vary. The survey results caused the students at South High School to be concerned. On the basis of their research, they considered second-hand smoke as a serious problem for asthmatic students, and they encouraged efforts to eliminate smoking in the homes of asthmatic students. Here again, it was important that they not imply that smoking *caused* asthma. Their study, based on the data from their all-school survey, did not show cause and effect but rather that the events "selecting a student with asthma" and "selecting a student living in a household with smokers" were not independent.

Solutions for "What's the Probability of a Hit?"

1. *a.* Four-tenths of the digits 0–9 represent hits for the player with a constant batting average of .400.
   b and *c.* The random digits 361, for example, would represent HNH, or "hit" followed by "no hit" followed by "hit." If the digits were 590, they would represent NNH, or two times at bat without a hit followed by an at-bat with a hit.

2. Students' answers to this question will vary, and it is appropriate to ask them to share their thinking about the number of sets of three at-bats in which the player would be likely to get at least 2 hits.

3. *a.* The sample space for three batting attempts is {HHH, HHN, HNH, NHH, HNN, NHN, NNH, NNN}. There are eight possible sequences of hits or "no hits."
   b. HHH, HHN, HNH, and NHH.
   c. Students' answers will vary.

4. *a.* The multiplication principle can be used to compute the probability of each of the eight individual outcomes. For example, $P(\text{HNH}) = (.4) \bullet (.6) \bullet (.4) = .096$.
   b. A tree diagram of all the outcomes for three at-bats with $P(\text{H}) = .4$ and $P(\text{N}) = .6$ is given in figure 4.3. The outcomes with at least two hits are HHH, HHN, HNH, and NHH. If X is the random variable *Number of hits in three at-bats,* then $P(X \geq 2) = P(\text{HHH}) + P(\text{HHN}) + P(\text{HNH}) + P(\text{NHH}) = (.4)^3 + 3 \bullet [(.4)^2 \bullet .6] = .352$.

5. *a* and *b*. Results will vary. One such run of 20 sets of 3 at-bats yielded the following: 3 hits occurred 1 time; 2 hits occurred 4 times; 1 hit occurred 11 times, 0 hits occurred 4 times. To get at least two hits in three times at bat, the batter must get either 2 hits or 3 hits. In these sample data, "at least two hits" occurred a total of 5 times in the 20 sets of three at-bats. In this case, the probability of at least two hits is 5/20, or .25.

   c and *d*. Results will vary.

6. Results will vary.

7. *a* and *b*. Results will vary. One such run of 50 sets of three at-bats yielded the following: 3 hits occurred 2 times; 2 hits occurred 12 times; 1 hit occurred 27 times, 0 hits occurred 9 times.

   c. Graphs will vary.

   d. In the sample data given in 7(*a* and *b*) above, "at least 2 hits" occurred a total of 14 times in the 50 sets of three at-bats. Thus, in this case, the probability of at least 2 hits is 14/50, or .28.

   e–g. Results will vary.

8. Comparisons among classmates should show a higher proportion of the probabilities within a tighter range in 50 simulations of three at-bats than in 20 simulations. Comparing data in this way can give students an opportunity to build connections between probability distributions and sampling distributions. (See *Navigating through Data Analysis in Grades 9–12* [Burrill et al. 2003].)

Solutions for "How Likely Is That Jury?"

1. *a*. $2^{12} = 4096$ total outcomes.

   b. The outcomes with 11 or more men are the members of the following set: {MMMMMMMMMMMM, WMMMMMMMMMMM, MWMMMMMMMMMM, MMWMMMMMMMMM, …, MMMMMMMMMMMW}. The set has thirteen members.

2. $(.5) \cdot (.5) \cdot (.5) \cdot \ldots \cdot (.5) = (.5)^{12} \approx .00024$.

3. *a*. There are thirteen outcomes with at least 11 men (see 1[*b*]). Each of these outcomes has a probability of $(.5)^{12}$ of occurring. Thus, $P(X \geq 11) \approx 13 \cdot .00024 \approx .003$, to three decimal places.

   b. Students can see that the probability of a randomly chosen jury with 11 or more men on it, assuming that men and women have equal chances of being selected for each place on the jury, is *very* small.

   c. Defendants and their lawyers who encounter such a situation should ask questions and support their objections with probability arguments.

4. *a–c*. Results will vary. Two runs of 40 tries yielded 0 such juries in one run, and 1 such jury in the other.

Solutions for "Consecutive Hits– Consecutively Hitless"

1. *a* and *b*. Students' answers will vary. Differences can give an opportunity for discussion and sharing of thinking. Questions like these are intended to improve students' intuitions about the chances of particular sequences of events before the students conduct a simulation or make a calculation to investigate the probabilities more closely.

2. *a–c*. Results will vary.

3. *a–c*. Results will vary.

4. *a*. $P(X = 4) = P(\text{NNNH}) = (.6) \cdot (.6) \cdot (.6) \cdot (.4) \approx .0864$

   b. $P(Y = 4) = P(\text{HHHN}) = (.4) \cdot (.4) \cdot (.4) \cdot (.6) \approx .0384$

c. Results will vary. Differences provide another opportunity for discussing and comparing the results of the simulations with the theoretical calculations.

Solutions for "One-Girl Family Planning"

1. Students' answers will vary.

2. Table 1 shows simulated data on 1026 children in 500 sibling groups formed under a one-girl policy of family planning. Here the mean number of children per sibling group is 1026 ÷ 500, or 2.05. If students use data from simulations of their own, their answers will vary depending on their simulated results. One sample solution is provided in the chapter discussion.

3. The partial probability distribution follows:

Number of Children in Sibling Group	Probability
1	.5
2	.25
3	$.125 \approx .13$
4	$.0625 \approx .06$
5	$.03125 \approx .03$
6	$.015625 \approx .02$
7	$.0078125 \approx .01$
8	$.00390625 \approx .00$
9	$.001953125 \approx .00$
10	$.0009765625 \approx .00$

4. *a* and *b.* Suppose there were 10000 sibling groups. Then you would expect $10000 \cdot .5 = 5000$ sibling groups of size 1, $10000 \cdot .25 = 2500$ sibling groups of size 2, etc. The mean number of children in these 10000 sibling groups is

$$\frac{5000 \cdot 1 + 2500 \cdot 2 + 1250 \cdot 3 + \ldots}{10000} \approx 2,$$

which should be very close to the mean number of children in the simulated families.

5. Yes, students should be able to express their work in the form $1 \cdot P(1) + 2 \cdot P(2) + 3 \cdot P(3) + \ldots$.

Solutions for "Shooting Free Throws"

1. Answers will vary, but most students will probably predict that making one successful shot is Lisa's most likely outcome on a one-and-one free-throw opportunity. Since Lisa's probability of making a successful free-throw shot is assumed to be .6, which is greater than her probability of missing a free throw (.4), most students will predict that making one successful shot (being successful on the first shot and the first shot only) is more likely than making no successful shots or making two successful shots.

2. In one possible simulation, students could use a random number table and assign the digits 1, 2, 3, 4, 5, and 6 to represent successful free throws and the digits 7, 8, 9, and 0 to represent missed free throws. Beginning on a randomly selected row of a random number table, they could let the leftmost digit represent Lisa's first shot. A 7, 8, 9, or 0 would mean that Lisa made zero successful shots on this one-and-one opportunity (in other words, her first shot missed, so she didn't get a chance at a second shot). Thus, any of the digits 7, 8, 9, or 0 would complete the first trial. However, a 1, 2, 3, 4, 5, or 6 would mean that Lisa made the first shot of the one-and-one, and students would need to look at the next digit in the row to determine the outcome of her second simulated shot. The

trial would be complete as soon as two simulated shots were successful or the second simulated shot was unsuccessful. Then students could move to the next digit in sequence to represent the first shot of Lisa's next one-and-one opportunity.

3. In the simulation just described, we can use random digits from lines 101 and 102 of table B in *The Practice of Statistics* (Yates, Moore, and Starnes 1999):

19223 95034 05756 28713 96409 12531 42544 82853

73676 47150 99400 01927 27754 42648 82425 36290

These digits simulate the following results:

Trial number	First digit	Second digit	Number of shots made
1	1	9	1
2	2	2	2
3	3	9	1
4	5	0	1
5	3	4	2
6	0	NA	0
7	5	7	1
8	5	6	2
9	2	8	1
10	7	NA	0
11	1	3	2
12	9	NA	0
13	6	4	2
14	0	NA	0
15	9	NA	0
16	1	2	2
17	5	3	2
18	1	4	2
19	2	5	2
20	4	4	2
21	8	NA	0
22	2	8	1
23	5	3	2
24	7	NA	0
25	3	6	2
26	7	NA	0
27	6	4	2
28	7	NA	0
29	1	5	2
30	0	NA	0
31	9	NA	0
32	9	NA	0
33	4	0	1
34	0	NA	0
35	0	NA	0
36	1	9	1
37	2	7	1
38	2	7	1
39	7	NA	0
40	5	4	2

A summary follows of the results of these simulations:

Number of shots made	0	1	2
Frequency	15	10	15

a. On the basis of the results of these trials, making one successful free throw is less likely than making zero or two successful free throws, and it appears that making no successful shots and making two successful shots are equally likely.

b. Answers will vary, depending on students' predictions in (1).

c. In the 40 simulated trials shown here, Lisa's mean number of successful free throws is

$$\frac{15 \cdot 0 + 10 \cdot 1 + 15 \cdot 2}{40}, \text{ or } 1.$$

4. a. P(Making 0 successful shots) $= .4$; P(Making 1 successful shot) $= (.6) \cdot (.4) = .24$; P(Making 2 successful shots) $= (.6) \cdot (.6) = .36$.

b. The expected value, or Lisa's mean number of points per one-and-one opportunity in the long run, is equal to $(0 \cdot .4) + (1 \cdot .24) + (2 \cdot .36) = .96$.

c. The theoretical value should be very close to the result from the simulation.

5. a. Answers will vary, but most students will predict that making one successful shot is the most likely outcome of a two-shot opportunity. Since Lisa's probability of making a free throw is assumed to be .6, students will usually expect Lisa to make about half her shots on the two-shot opportunities.

b. Usually, some students will predict that the mean number of free throws per two-shot opportunity will be $.6 \cdot 2$, or 1.2.

6. In one possible simulation, students could use a random-digit table and assign the digits 1, 2, 3, 4, 5, and 6 to represent successful free throws and the digits 7, 8, 9, and 0 to represent missed free throws. Taking a randomly selected row from the table, they could look at digits in pairs, beginning with the leftmost pair. The first digit in the pair would represent the outcome of the first free throw, and the second digit would represent the outcome of the second free throw. The digits in the first pair would thus simulate the outcome of the first trial. For the next trial, students would look at the second pair of digits. They would continue moving across and down the random digit table until they had examined 40 pairs of digits and recorded their results.

7. In the simulation just described, we can use lines 103 and 104 of table B in *The Practice of Statistics* (Yates, Moore, and Starnes 1999):

45467 71709 77558 00095 32863 29485 82226 90056

52711 38889 93074 60227 40011 85848 48767 52573

Trial Number	First digit	Second digit	Number of shots made	Trial Number	First digit	Second digit	Number of shots made
1	4	5	2	21	5	2	2
2	4	6	2	22	7	1	1
3	7	7	0	23	1	3	2
4	1	7	1	24	8	8	0
5	0	9	0	25	8	9	0
6	7	7	0	26	9	3	1
7	5	5	2	27	0	7	0
8	8	0	0	28	4	6	2
9	0	0	0	29	0	2	1
10	9	5	1	30	2	7	1
11	3	2	2	31	4	0	1
12	8	6	1	32	0	1	1
13	3	2	2	33	1	8	1
14	9	4	1	34	5	8	1
15	8	5	1	35	4	8	1
16	8	2	1	36	4	8	1
17	2	2	2	37	7	6	1
18	6	9	1	38	7	5	1
19	0	0	0	39	2	5	2
20	5	6	2	40	7	3	1

A summary follows of the results of these simulations:

Number of shots made	0	1	2
Frequency	9	20	11

a. On the basis of these 40 trials, making one successful shot is Lisa's most likely outcome in a two-shot free-throw opportunity.

b. Answers will vary, depending on students' predictions in 5(a).

c. In the 40 simulated trials shown here, Lisa's mean number of successful free throws is

$$\frac{9\cdot 0 + 20\cdot 1 + 11\cdot 2}{40} = 1.05.$$

d. Answers will vary, depending on students' predictions in 5(b).

8. a. P(Making 0 successful shots) $= .4 \bullet .4 = .16$, P(Making 1 successful shot) $= (.4 \bullet .6) + (.6 \bullet .4) = .48$, P(Making 2 successful shots) $= .6 \bullet .6 = .36$.

b. The expected value, or Lisa's mean number of points per two-shot opportunity in the long run, is equal to $(0 \bullet .16) + (1 \bullet .48) + (2 \bullet .36) = 1.20.$

c. The theoretical value should be very close to the result from the simulation.

9. The expected value per opportunity for one-and-one free throws is .96, and the expected value per opportunity for two-shot free throws is 1.20. Over the course of a season, this difference could prove to be very important for a player who gets fouled often.

Solutions for "39-Game Hitting Streak"

1. a. P(0 hits in 3 at-bats) $= (.6)^3 = .216.$
    P(at least 1 hit in 3 at bats) $= 1 - P(0 \text{ hits in 3 at-bats}) = 1 - (.6)^3 = .784$

b. P(1-game hitting streak) = P(at least 1 hit in first game and 0 hits in second game) = $(.784)(.216) \approx$ .16934 ≈ .17.

P(2-game hitting streak) = P(at least 1 hit in first game and at least 1 hit in second game and 0 hits in third game) = $(.784)(.784)(.216) \approx$ .13.

P(3-game hitting streak) = P(at least 1 hit in first game and at least 1 hit in second game and at least 1 hit in third game and 0 hits in fourth game) = $(.784)^3(.216) \approx$ .1.

c. P(39-game hitting streak) = $(.784)^{39}(.216) \approx$ .000016.

d. The ratio of these probabilities is

$$\frac{(.784)^3(.216)}{(.784)^{39}(.216)} = (.784)^{-36} \approx 6377.$$

It shows that a 3-game hitting streak, though not common for a player with a batting average like Molitor's, is much more likely than a 39-game streak.

2. *a.* In one possible simulation with a random number table, students could use any of the digits 1–4 to represent an at-bat that results in a hit and any of the digits 5–9 and 0 to represent an at-bat that does not result in a hit. Beginning on a randomly selected row of the random number table, they could look at digits in groups of three. Each digit in the group would represent a time at bat, and the three digits together would represent a single game with three at-bats. If any of the three digits were 1, 2, 3, or 4, then this game would have a hit. If these digits did not appear in the group of three, then the game would have no hit.

b. A summary follows of the results of 40 trials of the simulation:

Streak length	0	1	2	3	4	5	6	8	14
Frequency	12	10	3	5	2	3	2	2	1

3. *a.* The mean length of a hitting streak in the 40 trials was

$$\frac{12 \cdot 0 + 10 \cdot 1 + 3 \cdot 2 + 5 \cdot 3 + 2 \cdot 4 + 3 \cdot 5 + 2 \cdot 6 + 2 \cdot 8 + 1 \cdot 14}{40} = 2.4.$$

b. Students' answers will vary, depending on their simulated results.

4. P(at least 1 hit in 4 at-bats) = $1 - P$(0 hits in 4 at-bats) = $1 - (.6)^4 = .8704$.

P(39-game streak) = $(.8704)^{39}(.216) \approx .00058$.

5. In one possible simulation with a random number table, students could use any of the single digits 1–4 to represent an at-bat that results in a hit and any of the digits 5–9 and 0 to represent an at-bat that does not result in a hit. Beginning on a randomly selected row of the random number table, they could look at the digits in groups of four. Each digit in the group would represent the results of a time at bat, and the four digits together would represent a single game with four at-bats. If any of the four digits were 1, 2, 3, or 4, then this game would have a hit. If these digits did not appear in the group of four, then the game would have no hit.

A summary follows of the results of 40 trials of the simulation:

Streak length	0	1	2	3	4	5	6	7	10	12	13	16	17	25	41
Frequency	8	5	6	3	3	2	4	2	1	1	1	1	1	1	1

The mean length of a hitting streak in these 40 trials was

$$\frac{8 \cdot 0 + 5 \cdot 1 + 6 \cdot 2 + 3 \cdot 3 + 3 \cdot 4 + 2 \cdot 5 + 4 \cdot 6 + 2 \cdot 7 + 1 \cdot 10 + 1 \cdot 12 + 1 \cdot 13 + 1 \cdot 16 + 1 \cdot 17 + 1 \cdot 25 + 1 \cdot 41}{40} = 5.5.$$

6. This question provides an opportunity for a lively discussion about independent events. For additional material on the topic, see Larkey, Smith, and Kadane (1989) on the CD-ROM.

References

Burrill, Gail, Christine A. Franklin, Landy Godbold, and Linda J. Young. *Navigating through Data Analysis in Grades 9–12. Principles and Standards of School Mathematics* Navigations series. Reston, Va.: National Council of Teachers of Mathematics, 2003.

Gilovich, Thomas, Robert Vallone, and Amos Tversky. "The Hot Hand in Basketball: On the Misperception of Random Sequences." *Cognitive Psychology* 17 (July 1985): 295–314.

Hilsenrath, Joseph, and Bruce F. Field. "A Program to Simulate the Galton Quincunx." *Mathematics Teacher* 76 (November 1983): 571–73.

Hopfensperger, Patrick, Henry Kranendonk, and Richard Scheaffer. *Data-Driven Mathematics: Probability through Data.* White Plains, N.Y.: Dale Seymour Publications, 1999.

Konold, Clifford. "Teaching Probability through Modeling Real Problems." *Mathematics Teacher* 87 (April 1994): 232–35.

———. "Representing Probabilities with Pipe Diagrams." *Mathematics Teacher* 89 (May 1996): 378–82.

Konold, Clifford, and Craig D. Miller. Prob Sim (software). Amherst, Mass.: Statistics Education Research Group, University of Massachusetts, 1992.

Lappan, Glenda, Elizabeth Phillips, William M. Fitzgerald, and M. J. Winter. "Area Models and Expected Value." *Mathematics Teacher* 80 (November 1987): 650–54.

Larkey, Patrick D., Richard A. Smith, and Joseph B. Kadane. "It's Okay to Believe in the 'Hot Hand.'" *Chance* 2 (fall 1989): 22–30.

National Advisory Committee on Mathematical Education (NACOME). *Overview and Analysis of School Mathematics, Grades K–12.* Washington, D.C.: Conference Board of the Mathematical Sciences, 1975.

National Council of Teachers of Mathematics (NCTM). *An Agenda for Action: Recommendations for School Mathematics of the 1980s.* Reston, Va.: NCTM, 1980.

———. *Curriculum and Evaluation Standards for School Mathematics.* Reston, Va.: NCTM, 1989.

———. *Principles and Standards for School Mathematics.* Reston, Va.: NCTM, 2000.

Shaughnessy, J. Michael, and Michael Arcidiacono. *Visual Encounters with Chance: Math and the Mind's Eye,* Unit VIII. Salem, Ore.: The Math Learning Center, 1993.

Shaughnessy, J. Michael, and Judith S. Zawojewski, "Secondary Students' Performance on Data and Chance in the 1996 NAEP." *Mathematics Teacher* 92 (November 1999): 713–18.

Yates, Daniel S., David S. Moore, and Daren S. Starnes. *The Practice of Statistics.* New York: W. H. Freeman and Company, 1999.

Zawojewski, Judith S., and J. Michael Shaughnessy, "Data and Chance." In *Results from the Seventh Mathematics Assessment of the National Assessment of Educational Progress,* edited by Edward A. Silver and Patricia Ann Kenney, pp. 235–68. Reston, Va.: National Council of Teachers of Mathematics, 2000.

Suggested Reading

Bay, Jennifer M., Robert E. Reys, Ken Simms, and P. Mark Taylor. "Bingo Games: Turning Student Intuitions into Investigations in Probability and Number Sense." *Mathematics Teacher* 93 (March 2000): 200–206.

Chu, David, and Joan Chu. "A 'Simple' Probability Problem." *Mathematics Teacher* 85 (March 1992): 191–95.

Drake, Bob M. "Exploring Different Dice." *Mathematics Teacher* 86 (May 1993): 380–82.

Falk, Ruma. *Understanding Probability and Statistics: A Book of Problems.* Wellesley, Mass.: A K Peters, 1993.

Flores, Alfinio. "Connections: A Lottery, a Computer, and the Number *e*." *Mathematics Teacher* 86 (November 1993): 652–55.

Gross, Jay. "A Bernoulli Investigation." *Mathematics Teacher* 93 (December 2000): 756–57.

Haruta, Mako E., Mark Flaherty, Jean McGivney, and Raymond J. McGivney. "Coin Tossing." *Mathematics Teacher* 89 (November 1996): 642–45.

Hatfield, Larry. "Explorations with Chance." *Mathematics Teacher* 85 (April 1992): 280–82; 288–90.

Ippolito, Dennis. "The Spaghetti Problem Problem." *Mathematics Teacher* 93 (May 2000): 422–26.

Johnson, John M. "The Birthday Problem Explained." *Mathematics Teacher* 90 (January 1997): 20–22.

Jones, Kevin S. "The Birthday Problem Again?" *Mathematics Teacher* 86 (May 1993): 373–77.

Kiernan, James F. "Points on the Path to Probability." *Mathematics Teacher* 94 March 2001): 180–83.

Lesser, Lawrence M. "Exploring the Birthday Problem with Spreadsheets. *Mathematics Teacher* 92 (May 1999): 407–11.

Marks, Daniel. "The Big Loser." *Mathematics Teacher* 92 (March 1999): 208–13.

May, E. Lee, Jr. "Are Seven-Game Baseball Playoffs Fairer?" *Mathematics Teacher* 85 (October 1992): 528–31.

Mercer, Joseph O. "Some Surprising Probabilities from Bingo." *Mathematics Teacher* 86 (December 1993): 726–31.

Mosteller, Frederick. *Fifty Challenging Problems in Probability.* Reading, Mass.: Addison-Wesley Publishing, 1965.

Noone, Emeric T. "The Probability of Winning a Lotto Jackpot Twice." *Mathematics Teacher* 93 (September 2000): 519–20.

Pagni, Dave. "Playing 'Twenty Questions' with Attribute Blocks." *Mathematics Teacher* 86 (December 1993): 765–69.

Schielack, Vincent P., Jr. "The Football Coach's Dilemma: 'Should We Go for 1 or 2 Points First?'" *Mathematics Teacher* 88 (December 1995): 731–33.

Schwartzman, Steven. "An Unexpected Expected Value." *Mathematics Teacher* 86 (February 1993): 118–20.

Shaughnessy, J. Michael. "Connecting Research to Teaching: Probability and Statistics." *Mathematics Teacher* 86 (March 1993): 244–48.

Shi, Yixun. "A Mathematical Study of the Game 'Twenty-Four Points.'" *Mathematics Teacher* 92 (December 1999): 828–32.

Shulte, Albert P., ed. *Teaching Statistics and Probability*, 1981 Yearbook of the National Council of Teachers of Mathematics (NCTM). Reston, Va.: NCTM, 1981.

Teppo, Anne R., and Ted Hodgson. "Dinosaurs, Dinosaur Eggs, and Probability." *Mathematics Teacher* 94 (February 2001): 86–92.

Watson, Jane M. "Conditional Probability: Its Place in the Mathematics Curriculum." *Mathematics Teacher* 88 (January 1995): 12–17.

Wood, Eric. "Probability, Problem Solving, and 'The Price is Right.'" *Mathematics Teacher* 85 (February 1992): 103–9.

Woodward, Ernest, and Marilyn Woodward. "Expected Value and the Wheel of Fortune Game." *Mathematics Teacher* 87 (January 1994): 13–17.

Young, Paula Grafton. "Probability, Matrices, and Bugs in Trees." *Mathematics Teacher* 91 (May 1998): 402–5.